AF490750

60 DAYS TO FINDING JOY
IN THE EMPTY NEST

EMPTY NEST BLESSED

SUZY MICHELL

EMPTY NEST BLESSED

SUZY MIGHELL

Table of Contents

I'm so happy you're here!

Ten years ago, when our youngest child left the nest, I found myself asking, "Now what?" I longed to do something meaningful, purposeful, and—most of all— helpful to others. In short, I wanted to be a blessing.

For years, I'd poured myself into encouraging, teaching, speaking, and leading women, both professionally and personally. My joyful spirit, can-do attitude, and faith have always been woven into everything I do and share. But suddenly, with my active parenting days behind me, I felt adrift. One minute, I was grieving the close of a beloved chapter. The next minute, I was giddy with the realization that I had the freedom to write a whole new one. Do you relate?

That season drove me straight to my knees. I asked the Lord, "How do You want me to use this new chapter? How can I be a blessing now?"

As I looked around, I realized I wasn't alone. Many of my friends were floundering too, mourning the shift in their roles as moms and feeling unsure about how to refocus on themselves after years of pouring into others. Health, fitness, fashion, faith, friendships, even purpose… it was all on the table. But where to start? And why did it feel so *awkward* to put ourselves first? (Spoiler alert: We'd been putting others first for eighteen-plus years!)

I was right there, figuring it out day by day, prayer by prayer. And that's when the Lord planted a desire in my heart to encourage, uplift, and cheer on my fellow empty nesters. Could I share my journey and let God use it for good? Could I be brave enough to say, "Here's what I'm learning. Come along with me?"

I had a dear friend who had started a successful blog, and I floated my idea by her: a space for women navigating the empty nest. She loved it! Her encouragement was like a spark to the fire already burning in my heart.

The Lord gave me the name *Empty Nest Blessed*, and it said everything I hoped this season could be. My family loved it too, and their excitement gave me the confidence to move forward.

There was just one small problem: I didn't know how to do anything "techie." (Like, at all!) I had to figure out how to register a domain, build a website, brand myself, create a logo, apply for a trademark… and that's just the beginning. It was overwhelming! But I kept moving forward, step by step, sure that I was walking in God's purpose and plan.

To my surprise, I didn't feel old or out of place as
I learned. Instead, I found YouTube videos, kind
customer service reps, and tech experts who patiently
explained it all. Their kindness encouraged me and
reminded me that I wasn't too late—I was right on
time.

Six months later, I published my first blog post. It
was about adjusting to the empty nest. The next
one was about finding purpose. I kept writing, and
EmptyNestBlessed.com kept growing. I shared about
cooking for two, our empty-nester travels, rediscovering
my sense of style, my health and fitness journey, and
even how I was handling those new little wrinkles on
my face.

To my amazement and delight, women from all over
the world responded.

In the ten years since beginning this journey, I've
had the joy of connecting with thousands of women
through blog posts, speaking engagements, media
interviews, social media, and sometimes even in person!
Every message, every comment, every story shared has
been a blessing.

That brings me to this book.

*Empty Nest Blessed: 60 Days to Finding Joy in the Empty
Nest* was born out of those conversations with you,

my fellow empty nesters. I wanted to write a book that didn't feel intimidating or overwhelming. So, I broke it down into sixty bite-sized, grace-filled days of encouragement and action. Each chapter is designed to inspire you, equip you, and give you simple, practical steps to take—one day at a time.

Together, we'll explore everything from discovering purpose and cultivating joy to navigating your relationship with adult kids, reigniting your passions, and embracing the freedom of this beautiful season.

There will be challenges, of course. But, oh, friend—there will be JOYS.

There will be growth. There will be laughter. There will be purpose. And yes, there will be fun!

Parenting is a sacred calling. And while it never truly ends, the transition to the empty nest is a significant life shift. My prayer is that this book brings joy and hope to your heart, and that you'll feel me beside you, cheering you on and saying, "You've got this, and I'm right here with you."

The Lord has a plan for this season of your life. Let's discover it together.

WHO ARE YOU NOW?

Who Are You?

**Before I formed you in the womb I
knew you, before you were born I
set you apart; I appointed you as a
prophet to the nations.**

Jeremiah 1:5 (NIV)

I want you to do something for me. It's going to sound kind of crazy, but I want you to do it anyway.

Write down ten words that describe you.

Next, I want you to text ten people you know well—including your kids—and ask them to describe you in **three** words. (You might preface the question by telling them that you're doing something *weird*, and that you would appreciate it if they would not ask questions!)

Ask them not to think too deeply about the words. Instead, just send the three words that immediately come to mind.

When I was a new empty nester, doing this exercise was a light bulb moment for me! I thought I'd get words like "bossy" or "opinionated." But instead, I got words like "directed," "encouraging," "confident," and "organized."

So often, we don't see ourselves the way others see us! Figuring out how others thought of me was helpful and encouraging as I sought to move forward as an empty nester.

(It turns out God wanted me to be an encourager of others as my actual job!)

Use the space below to record the words you receive. You're going to want to come back to this to remind yourself who you are in the eyes of those who love you and know you best.

And I will be a Father to you, and you shall be sons and daughters to me, says the Lord Almighty.

2 Corinthians 6:18

Even if you had a high-powered career or other commitments that kept you busy, the day you gave birth, being a mother became your *primary identity*.

That's a good thing, and it means that you were probably a devoted and loving mom! In fact, you may even find that you were so used to being a mom and putting others first that you don't really know *yourself* anymore. It's **normal** to wonder who you are now that you're not needed as a mom on a day-to-day basis.

How do you see yourself? Is your identity in your role as a mother, a wife, a daughter, a business owner, or some other role?

Remember, you were a *woman* before you were ever a *mother*. Mothering is a sacred task, to be sure, but

before you became a mother, you were a woman imbued by God with talents, skills, hobbies, interests, and abilities. A big part of adjusting to and finding purpose in the empty nest is reconnecting with that woman.

She's still there—and guess what? She's better than ever. You brought skills and abilities into mothering that made you a better mother. And as you mothered, you learned additional skills that helped you fulfill that role well. (Think chef, chauffeur, counselor, tutor, medical diagnostician, driving instructor, and lots more!)

Think of the skills and abilities you brought into mothering. Write those down. Next, add those you learned as a mother. The Lord has been at work in you, and He's got big plans for your future! (Jeremiah 29:11)

But Who Are You, REALLY?

**I have called you by name;
you are mine.**

Isaiah 43:1b

As important as it is to go through exercises like determining how others see you and figuring out who *you* believe you are, it's also important to remember that what others see is an outgrowth of who you are inside. **Your heart is your true self.** Think of Proverbs 4:23: *Above all else, guard your heart, for everything you do flows from it.*

How is your heart doing? Who does your heart say that you are? A mother? An empty nester? A wife? An employee?

The truth is, our identity isn't found in a role we play, or even in the opinions of others—it's found in God and who He says we are. When we align our daily lives with His truth about our identity, it functions like a plumb line, keeping us oriented toward who we actually are in the eyes of the One who made us and who guides our every step.

You don't hear much about plumb lines these days, so I'll explain! A plumb line is a simple but powerful tool. It's a weighted string that hangs straight down, using gravity to find the perfect vertical line. Builders and interior designers use it to ensure things are perfectly aligned, but it's also an excellent metaphor for life! Just like how a plumb line keeps structures standing tall and straight, we need to get our bearings in life by keeping our eyes focused on who *He* says we are.

The truth is, our identity isn't found in a role we play, or even in the opinions of others—it's found in God and who He says we are.

In His Word, we can begin to see ourselves the way He sees us: loved, valued, and created with a purpose, among other things. God not only created you but also formed you and called you to serve Him. The people (including your children) and experiences (including trials) He's brought into your life have made you the person you are today.

You were made for a purpose; you are His; and He's not finished with you yet! He has a plan for this season of your life, and the way to start uncovering that plan is to first have a firm grasp on who you (really) are! Do you see yourself the way He sees you—deeply loved, purposefully created, and fully known?

Those three words describing you that your ten people texted? They're good to know, but they're *not* your plumb line.

Do you know and fully grasp who He says you are? Take some time to go through the list provided and use the space below to write down the ones you need to remember.

50 Things God Says About You

1. He has called you by name, and you are His.
   – Isaiah 43:1b

2. You are loved with an everlasting love.
   – Jeremiah 31:3

3. You are created in His image.
   – Genesis 1:27

4. You are fearfully and wonderfully made.
   – Psalm 139:14

5. You are known by Him.
   – Jeremiah 1:5

6. You are deeply loved.
   – Romans 8:38–39

7. You are His masterpiece.
   – Ephesians 2:10

8. You are chosen.
   – 1 Peter 2:9

9. You are His child.
    – John 1:12

10. You are redeemed.
    – Colossians 1:13–14

11. You are forgiven.
    – 1 John 1:9

12. You are a new creation.
    – 2 Corinthians 5:17

13. You are set apart.
    – Jeremiah 1:5

14. You are His temple.
    – 1 Corinthians 6:19

15. You are complete in Christ.
    – Colossians 2:10

16. You are free from
    condemnation.
    – Romans 8:1

17. You are a friend of Jesus.
    – John 15:15

18. You are more than a
    conqueror.
    – Romans 8:37

19. You are light in the world.
    – Matthew 5:14

20. You are the salt of the
    earth.
    – Matthew 5:13

21. You are never alone.
    – Hebrews 13:5

22. You are His workmanship.
    – Ephesians 2:10

23. You are sealed with the
    Holy Spirit.
    – Ephesians 1:13

24. You are an heir with Christ.
    – Romans 8:17

25. You are strengthened
    by Him.
    – Philippians 4:13

26. You are victorious in Christ.
    – 1 Corinthians 15:57

27. You are wonderfully made
    for a purpose.
    – Ephesians 2:10

28. You are a citizen of heaven.
    – Philippians 3:20

29. You are never forgotten.
    – Isaiah 49:15–16

30. You are hidden with Christ
    in God.
    – Colossians 3:3

31. You are born of God.
    – 1 John 5:18

32. You are being transformed.
    – 2 Corinthians 3:18

33. You are a daughter
    of the King.
    – 2 Corinthians 6:18

34. You are delivered from the
    power of darkness.
    – Colossians 1:13

35. You are blessed with every
    spiritual blessing.
    – Ephesians 1:3

36. You are an ambassador
    for Christ.
    – 2 Corinthians 5:20

37. You are part
    of a royal priesthood.
    – 1 Peter 2:9

38. You are precious
    in His sight.
    – Isaiah 43:4

39. You are held securely
    in His hand.
    – John 10:28

40. You are justified by faith.
    – Romans 5:1

41. You are called to do
    good works.
    – Matthew 5:16

42. You are clothed with
    strength and dignity.
    – Proverbs 31:25

43. You are saved by grace
    through faith.
    – Ephesians 2:8

44. You are being renewed
    day by day.
    – 2 Corinthians 4:16

45. You are a co-laborer
    with Christ.
    – 1 Corinthians 3:9

46. You are filled with
    the Holy Spirit.
    – 1 Corinthians 3:16

47. You are never forsaken.
    – Deuteronomy 31:6

48. You are called to peace.
    – Colossians 3:15

49. You are protected by
    His power.
    – 1 Peter 1:5

50. You are secure
    in His love.
    – Romans 8:35–39

You're Amazing!

**There is a time for everything,
and a season for every activity
under the heavens.**

Ecclesiastes 3:1 (NIV)

How old are you? How old do you feel? Who cares?

If you're an empty nester, you're a survivor! You lived through the days of no bike helmets, no seat belts, and drinking out of garden hoses, among other shocking things! Those gray hairs you're starting to see? They're your crown, Queen! Those crow's feet? They show that you've loved well and laughed much. That extra skin around your middle testifies to a miracle: it shows that you grew *life* inside your body.

It seems like our society sees aging as a problem that needs to be cured, fixed, erased, and resisted. We hear the voices that say aging is about fading, slowing down, and becoming less relevant. But we know the truth!

This season is about stepping into strength, wisdom, and the women that our life experiences have shaped us to be. There are incredible possibilities still ahead! While the world may whisper that aging means losing value, we know better—we're more confident, capable, and full of purpose than ever before.

You are absolutely *amazing*.

- You created a home! Whether big or small, you made a space filled with love and memories.

- You poured into people—family, friends, church, community— serving them by offering support and encouragement.

- You grew in faith, wisdom, and resilience as you navigated life's challenges with strength, wisdom, and grace.

- You nurtured, guided, and loved your children into adulthood. That's no small feat!

- You cultivated deep, long-lasting friendships.

- You developed a career and grew in your abilities. (Whether you worked inside or outside the home, trust me, your contributions made a difference!)

- You're embracing change. Life looks different now, and you're adjusting, learning, and working to find joy in the new season.

I'm celebrating the Lord's faithfulness in your life, and I'm *so* proud of you!

Use the space below to list some of the things
you've accomplished in your life, with the Lord's
help. Do you realize you're well-prepared for
whatever God has in store for you in the next
season of your life?

PREPARING FOR THE EMPTY NEST

Nobody Likes Change

Jesus Christ is the same yesterday and today and forever.

Hebrews 13:8 (NIV)

Without a doubt, entering the empty nest season of life can be a complex time of transition. Not only are you dealing with the adjustment to the empty nest, but this time is often accompanied by a milestone birthday.

Throw in the physical changes of midlife, adjusting to an empty-nest marriage (or, if you're single, possibly resuming dating!), learning to reframe the relationship you have with your (now-adult) kids, the challenges of redefining yourself as a woman in today's world, and more. Oh, it's *a lot*.

I turned fifty on the *exact* day I dropped my last child off at college. Seriously? As I drove away in tears, I remember thinking, *What just happened?* The weight of it all was almost too much to bear, but I remember being comforted by the knowledge that, although everything in my life was changing and I felt completely unmoored, my Savior was unchanging.

Remember, just like in any other season of life, the blessings of the empty nest accompany the challenges.

First, you're adjusting to the empty nest itself, which is a *significant* life transition. But you're *also* working to make another significant adjustment—giving yourself (guilt-free) permission to focus on many of the areas of life you may have set aside while busy with child-rearing.

Remember, just like any other season of life, the blessings of the empty nest accompany the challenges.

The focus-on-yourself muscles may have atrophied with a lack of use as you focused on your children! But now, it's time to start flexing, stretching, and working out those muscles.

Mama, it's *your* time!

What changes are you struggling with right now? What areas of life do you need to give yourself permission to focus on now that the kids are out of the nest? Use the space below to make a list and find one specific thing you can do today that's just for yourself. (I'm giving you permission!)

**A word fitly spoken is like apples of
gold in a setting of silver.**

Proverbs 25:11

It's time, my friend! If you haven't already done it,
it's time to talk with your college-bound teen or new
college student about expectations for communication,
among other things. You need to come to an agreement
on things like how often to text, call, or video chat.

How will both of you handle it if one of you isn't able
to respond to a text or voicemail right away? Does that
go both ways? The answer to that question surprised
me!

While I expected that I would be the one anxiously
waiting for a return text, I found that after years of
having me close at hand, it was the other way around!
I got lots of texts and voicemails from my just-out-of-
the-nest kids saying things like, "Where *are* you? I *need*

to talk to you!"

How often does your child anticipate coming home for weekends? Will that visit home involve laundry? Who's going to do that laundry?

Who's paying for what? Is there a plan for unexpected expenses that may pop up?

While having these types of discussions before the actual departure date (when everyone's emotions are running high) is helpful, if you're already past that point and haven't had these conversations, it's okay. But it does need to be done.

Discussing expectations and planning in a time of low stress and non-conflict is ideal. Don't wait until emotions may be riding high. Remember that the decisions you make aren't set in stone! It's okay to say something like, "Let's try this, and revisit things in a couple of months to see how it's going."

Have the conversations you need to have as soon as possible and get everyone on the same page.

What crucial conversations do you need to have with your young adult kids? Use the lines below to jot down the issues you need to address and make a plan for when to address them.

I Second That Emotion

**So do not fear, for I am with you; do
not be dismayed, for I am your God.
I will strengthen you and help you;
I will uphold you with my righteous
right hand.**

Isaiah 41:10 (NIV)

You're probably feeling a complex mix of emotions
as you face the empty nest phase of your life. It's a
significant life change, and what you're feeling is totally
normal! After eighteen-plus years of focusing on the
life-altering task of raising a child, letting that child go
is not as easy as just flipping a light switch. It's a process
and a significant life transition.

But who else is facing a big life change right now? *Your
child!*

Just as you have feelings of uncertainty about life as an
empty nester, your son or daughter has similar feelings

about leaving home. Do you remember how you felt? Be there to listen and offer reassurance without giving advice, or even "suggestions."

When it comes to your own emotions, remember that *you* are the adult. You don't want to increase your son or daughter's anxiety by imposing your own emotional neediness on them. That would be selfish and unkind.

Be careful! Sometimes you can share your feelings unintentionally in a way that could be guilt-inducing or emotionally taxing to them. For example, telling them repeatedly how much you are going to miss them may seem like a loving way to show them how important they are to you, but it can communicate the message that your happiness is dependent on them. That's a lot of unhealthy pressure to impose!

Your child is not responsible for your happiness. Instead, focus on them and work on instilling confidence in them. Say things like, "You've got this!" or "You're ready! Go get 'em."

Are you more focused on your child's emotions or your own? Remember to finish strong as a parent! Focus on *them*. There will be time later to deal with your emotions. Use the space below to jot down how you might need to adjust as you get them ready to go.

**Our mouths were filled with laughter,
our tongues with songs of joy.**

Psalm 126:2

If you feel, well, kinda *happy* about the prospect of an empty nest, that's awesome! In fact, it's *normal* to feel a sense of relief and even newfound energy as you look forward. Don't feel guilty about this! Life as an empty nester can be invigorating!

My husband has a motto for the empty nest season of life. He says, "We can do what we want, when we want, for as long as we want!" While those sentiments might not always ring *entirely* true, there *are* some wonderful things about the empty nest season of life.

I remember feeling almost giddy at times when I thought about my newfound freedom to go and do things without having to consider my kids and their activities. However, those feelings were often accompanied by feelings of guilt. It felt wrong to feel that way, as if I didn't love my kids enough.

Thankfully, an older empty nester set me straight.

She reminded me that feeling happy and excited about being an empty nester didn't mean I loved my children any less. In fact, it was healthy and appropriate! After all, I wanted my kids to be happy and excited about the next phase of their lives. Your child is stepping into a new season of life, filled with fresh experiences! Take a cue from them and do the same!

So go ahead! Get your happy on! It's okay!

What makes you excited about life as an empty nester? Make a list below and thank God for those things.

THE NEST EMPTIES

Good Grief

**The Lord is near to the brokenhearted
and saves the crushed in spirit.**

Psalm 34:18

Grief plays an underacknowledged role in the empty-nest transition. After all, shifting to an empty nest is a profound life change! Feeling emotions like sadness and loss is normal. It's okay to cry! Crying can be a stress reliever and a healthy way to express emotions.

I remember sitting in my son's room sobbing the day after he left. Lots of moms tell me they've done this. My feelings of grief were acute in those first days, and I would get teary at random moments, but the grief *gradually* waned over the first two months of life as an empty nester.

Give yourself permission to feel sadness without judgment. Acknowledge and lean into your emotions, working through them. If you're married, talk with your spouse about your feelings. (Chances are they share many of the same ones!) If you're a single parent, talk with friends and family about this life transition.

Most likely, you'll find sympathy and understanding. If needed, seek out a pastor or a licensed counselor.

Know that if you're predisposed to depression, empty nest grief *may* trigger it. If you find that you're unable to get out of bed, shower, or resume activities you enjoy, or if you're abusing substances like alcohol to cope, you need to seek help.

What can be confusing is that *some* parents don't seem to deal with grief when they become empty nesters! Although you may simultaneously feel a joyful sense of newfound freedom with grief, for some parents, there doesn't seem to be any sense of sadness at all!

Don't judge or worry about how others are dealing with the transition. Just lean into *your* feelings and *own* them. Work through them in your own time and in your own way.

LIVE IT OUT

Where are you on the emotion scale right now? If one is gleeful and ten is heartbroken, where do you fall? Write a few sentences about how you're feeling emotionally and how it relates to the number you selected. Monitor this as time goes on, and make sure you're trending upward.

1   2   3   4   5   6   7   8   9   10

**I will restore to you the years
that the swarming locust has eaten,
the hopper, the destroyer, and
the cutter, my great army, which
I sent among you.**

Joel 2:25

Are you behind on a few things? It's okay!

When my nest emptied, I had to face up to the fact
that I'd been using the busyness of raising my kids as
an excuse to neglect some areas in my life that needed
attention.

I admitted to myself that I needed to do a better job of
learning technology, so I wouldn't have to ask my kids
for help constantly. I also knew I was behind on some
of my vaccinations. ("My last tetanus shot, doctor? I
have no idea!") I knew my aging parents needed more
of my time and attention.

Are there things you may have put off during the years of focusing on your children? You know in your heart what you need to work on, so be honest with yourself.

- ☐ Yearly physicals

- ☐ Diagnostic tests

- ☐ Vaccinations

- ☐ Dental Health

- ☐ Physical Fitness

- ☐ Nutrition

- ☐ Spiritual Life

- ☐ Technology

- ☐ Wardrobe

- ☐ Skin

- ☐ Organization

- ☐ Relationships (spouse, parents, siblings, friends)

Make a plan to address these things. Sometimes "later" can become "never," so do it now!

Do you need to join a gym or find a personal trainer? Has it been a while since you've visited the dentist? Do you have beauty issues that you want to address? Does your wardrobe need an update?

Resist feeling overwhelmed. Take it one task at a time. And remember, you're not alone! There are experts who can help you take steps in the right direction, so you'll have someone guiding you and cheering you on. I know from talking to thousands of empty nesters—all of them feel this way to some extent!

It's time to make necessary changes and updates. It takes courage to ask for help, but you can do it. I believe in you!

Prioritize! Then use the to-do list below to make some appointments and start working your way through your list.

- [ ]
- [ ]
- [ ]
- [ ]
- [ ]
- [ ]
- [ ]
- [ ]
- [ ]
- [ ]
- [ ]
- [ ]

Get While the Getting's Good

The Lord had said to Abram, 'Go from your country, your people and your father's household to the land I will show you.'

Genesis 12:1 (NIV)

Let's be real. Parenting is basically the business of working yourself out of a job. When your child graduates from high school and goes off to college, it's a cause for celebration. (Good job! This is what you've been working toward!) You need to celebrate the closing of a significant chapter in your life and anticipate the joy of what is to come during the next season.

When I speak to empty nesters, this next suggestion surprises and delights them! Here it comes…

Make travel arrangements for a trip sometime within your first few months as an empty nester. It will give you something to plan for and look forward to during that initial period of adjustment. I recommend somewhere you've never been and have always wanted to go to. It doesn't need to be overly expensive or exotic, but this is not the time to head to your family lake house for a long weekend!

As an empty nester, you don't need to vacation when everyone else is vacationing because you're not tied to a school schedule, so it's easy to take advantage of affordable off-season travel!

The good news is that September and October are great months for empty nesters to find travel deals. That coincides perfectly with kids going back to school!

Ever heard of "shoulder season?" It's the season between the peak and off-peak seasons. During shoulder season, prices are usually significantly less than during peak season, yet the weather conditions are very similar. I like to call it "Empty Nester Season!"

When we planned our first empty-nester getaway, I told my husband we needed to stay somewhere nearby. After all, our daughter might need us! This makes me laugh now, but at the time, I was dead serious! News flash: she didn't!

The kids will be fine! Now, where do you want to go? Get planning!

Use the lines below to make a list of possible destinations. Then search for deals and start planning!

"Blessed is he who expects nothing,
for he shall never be disappointed."[1]

Alexander Pope

I'm just going to come right out and say it. *Unrealistic expectations will steal your joy.*

Blame social media, movies, or whatever, but we all have some sort of idea in our minds of how happy and stable families are supposed to look and feel. Sweet friend, *nobody's* family looks like that perfect one that lives in your mind!

Expectations have a way of setting us up for disappointment, especially when they're unrealistic (which, let's be real, they usually are). Whether we realize it or not, we all have an idea of how our kids' college breaks *should* unfold. We tend to script in our minds how things will go when our kids come home— how much time we'll spend together, the conversations

we'll have, the special moments we'll share. But here's the truth: No one can live up to that perfect plan—not you, not your kids.

As I talk to empty-nester mamas, I see it time and again—expectations can be one of our biggest challenges. They shape how we think our kids will handle life outside the nest, how we believe we'll feel in this new season, and even how we imagine their visits home will go. But even when they seem reasonable, expectations have a way of stealing our joy. Because the truth is, real life rarely unfolds exactly as we picture it.

Instead of holding onto a picture-perfect vision that is entirely unrealistic, focus on what really matters and embrace the moments with gratitude in your heart as they come. Rather than placing expectations on others, put them on yourself.

When my adult children are home, my expectations for myself are always the same:

1. To make our home and family a fun
   and positive place where they love to
   spend time.

2. To create a safe environment where
   they feel *heard*, and where I can build
   them up and encourage them.

Ideally, having those **two clear-cut goals** will impact
every word out of my mouth and everything I do. (That
doesn't always happen, but I pray about it constantly
and try my best!)

Have you set expectations for your growing kids that are unrealistic and even unfair? Be honest and write those down. Then draw a big X over them and, instead, write out some goals and expectations for yourself.

1. EXPECTATIONS I'VE PLACED ON MY KIDS

We Were on a Break

**He heals the brokenhearted and
binds up their wounds.**

Psalm 147:3 (NIV)

Anyone who has experienced loss understands the ebb
and flow of grief. One of the things no one talks about
in the empty nest is how, in the beginning, you may
feel a resurgence of empty nest grief every time your
kids come home for a visit, only to leave again. It's okay.
I promise it will get better over time, but in those early
months, it's common to feel that way.

When I became an empty nester, nothing prepared me
for how I would feel after Christmas break. I thought
I had moved past the grief! We were beginning to
really enjoy the empty nest... until the kids left after
being home for the holidays. Suddenly, those complex
emotions resurfaced. After talking to other empty-
nester moms, I was relieved to learn that these feelings
were completely normal.

Not only did I mistakenly assume my kids would want to spend lots of time with me while they were home (*expectations!*), but I also hadn't considered the challenges that would come up after months of them living independently. Rules? Curfew? Nope. Independence? Yep. And guess what? That's normal and appropriate, though it was a little jarring at first.

Still, I missed them terribly when they left to go back to school. Even years later, when they leave after visiting, it can feel like someone has sucked all the air out of the room. I miss their energy. (Although, at the same time, I'm also a little relieved to have the peace and quiet back!)

Of course, not everyone struggles with this rebound grief! After speaking to a group of moms on this topic, one mom approached me afterward with a story. Her college student had just taken a semester of Psychology 101 and spent his Christmas break "diagnosing" family members and analyzing family dynamics. She had expected to grieve when he left to go back to school, but *somehow*, she didn't feel sad at all!

Jot down the dates for upcoming breaks below. Thinking ahead and praying about these times can help you manage the feelings that may accompany them.

JANUARY

S	M	T	W	T	F	S

FEBRUARY

S	M	T	W	T	F	S

MARCH

S	M	T	W	T	F	S

APRIL

S	M	T	W	T	F	S

MAY

JUNE

JULY

AUGUST

SEPTEMBER

OCTOBER

NOVEMBER

DECEMBER

Welcome Home! The Dos & Don'ts

Therefore, as God's chosen people, holy and dearly loved, clothe yourselves with compassion, kindness, humility, gentleness, and patience.

Colossians 3:12 (NIV)

Whether they're back for a quick weekend visit, for the holidays, or for summer break, at some point those little adults will be back in the nest, and it will be clear that the rules of engagement have changed! You'll be trying to figure out how, and frankly, so will they!

This is the time for patience, grace, and open communication. This is not the time to be quick to take offense or be overly sensitive.

Here's a rundown of some basic dos and don'ts:

DO

- Talk about the visit beforehand to set expectations. (What's the plan?)

- Create a warm, welcoming, and fun environment!

- Welcome them with their favorite snacks!

- Respect their independence. (They've been living on their own and making their own decisions.)

- Show unconditional love. (Kids of every age crave it!)

- Find things to encourage. (See my list for suggestions!)

- Let them be the "expert."

- Be a good listener.

- Wait for them to bring up personal issues, like dating.

- Give them space.

- Let them sleep. (They may be exhausted!)

- Thank them for coming home to visit and tell them it meant a lot to you.

- Give advice or even "suggestions" without being asked.

- Expect them to fall back into old routines.

- Forget your goal. (You're working to *transition* your relationship to friendship.)

- Overload their schedules.

- Be afraid to set boundaries if needed.

- Go into the visit with a huge agenda.

- Shift conversations to yourself. Stay focused on them.

- Criticize their friends.

- Make them feel guilty about leaving. (Don't say things like, "You're leaving already?")

- Forget to enjoy the moment!

Got a visit coming up on the calendar? Use the space below to jot down some notes, to-dos, or things you want to remember.

Full House, Full Heart

**So he got up and went to his father.
But while he was still a long way off,
his father saw him and was filled
with compassion for him; he ran to
his son, threw his arms around him
and kissed him.**

Luke 15:20 (NIV)

When your empty nest fills up for the holidays or the summer, it's an adjustment. Not only is your peaceful, quiet, clean nest upended, but your workload multiplies.

But if you're like me, *none* of that matters! When your empty nest fills up again, your focus is on your kids, and your joy at having your chicks home to roost is boundless. So, how can you make the most of the time you have with your adult kids?

1. **Be Intentional**:

Think about your time with your kids. How can you strengthen relationships and build intimacy? What are your goals? How do you plan to accomplish them?

2. **Adjust Your Expectations**:

Unrealistic expectations are thieves of joy. We tend to make assumptions about how our interactions and conversations will go. *This is dangerous business!* Don't fall for it. Instead, resolve to go with the flow.

3. **Focus on Gratitude**:

Set your mind and heart on gratitude for each moment you have together. You'll see signs of newfound maturity in your child. Rejoice!

4. **Be Positive and Radiate Joy**:

You want your adult children to think of your home as a warm and loving place they want to visit. Create that environment!

5. **Be a Good Friend**:

If you want to stay relevant and important in their lives, you need to learn to be a good friend to them! Good friends are *good listeners*; they *ask good questions*; they are *respectful, encouraging, supportive,* and *thoughtful.* They *don't give advice without being asked.* If you want your kids to think of you as their friend, you'll need to be the kind of friend they enjoy being around and can trust with their hearts.

6. **Keep Your Sense of Humor**:

Don't take yourself too seriously! Be quick to laugh at situations that occur, mishaps that arise, and especially at *yourself.* Laughter makes everything better.

7. **Lean on Your Support System**:

There will be times when you need to talk through a situation or even vent over the holidays. That's totally normal. I rely on my faith, my husband and friends, and sometimes even deep breathing exercises when things get exasperating!

If you want your kids to think of you as their friend, you'll need to be the kind of friend they enjoy being around and can trust with their hearts.

Be thoughtful and intentional about upcoming times when your kids will be home. Use the space below to jot down the things you need to think and pray about before they arrive.

Worry Wart

**Do not be anxious about anything,
but in every situation, by prayer and
petition, with thanksgiving, present
your requests to God. And the
peace of God, which transcends all
understanding, will guard your hearts
and your minds in Christ Jesus.**

Philippians 4:6–7

It's *normal* to worry about your kids once they're gone. Will they be able to take care of themselves on their own? Do they have the necessary skills to adult successfully? Will they stay safe and make good decisions? Did I teach them everything they needed to know? (Spoiler alert: No!)

For me, worrying often gets mixed up with regret. I think back on the years gone by and wish I'd done a few (or many) things differently. I find myself regretting parenting decisions I made, and think, "If only I'd ___________________." (Fill in the blank with "worked less," "been stricter," "been more supportive," etc.)

We all feel that way sometimes! When I was moving my then twenty-six-year-old son into his post-college apartment, I started mentally beating myself up that I hadn't done a better job of teaching him to clean and cook.

The truth is, there is only one perfect parent. I had to remember that I did the best I could and let it go.

Worry and regret can leave you feeling helpless. But guess what? God doesn't want you to feel that way! You're far from helpless! We're told in 1 Peter 5:7, *Cast all your anxiety on Him, for He cares for you.*

"Casting" is an *active verb!* (Picture a fisherman casting his line out into the water.) God promises His peace. Train yourself to cast whenever those worries overtake your thoughts. And then cast again. And again. He's got this.

Write out your worries on the next page. Then cast those worries on the Lord, tear out that page, and throw it away.

I Choose Joy

Go and enjoy choice food and sweet
drinks, and send some to those who
have nothing prepared. This day is
holy to our Lord. Do not grieve, for
the joy of the Lord is your strength.

Nehemiah 8:10 (NIV)

Are you struggling to find **joy** in the empty nest?

Joy is not the same thing as happiness. Happiness is an emotion. Emotions are our natural responses to life's events, circumstances, and situations. While we may love the high we get from happiness, true **joy** is steady and dependable. It's not dependent on circumstances.

Years ago, I decided to do a study of the word "**joy**" in the Bible. It took a long time because I literally looked up *every single mention* to **joy** in scripture and wrote down what the Bible said about it. I almost filled up an entire notebook!

Guess what I found over and over again? **Joy** almost always goes hand-in-hand with gratitude!

Because **joy**, and by default gratitude, are muscles that get stronger with use, if you want to pursue **joy**, you're going to have to be intentional about practicing gratitude and cultivating a heart of **joy**.

What does this look like practically?

First of all, since you can't know how to get somewhere without knowing where you're going, if you're serious about wanting more **joy** in your life, I recommend that you do a study of the word "**joy**" in the Bible as I did. Knowing and understanding what God says about **joy** is really the key to cultivating it.

Because joy, and by default gratitude, are muscles that get stronger with use, if you want to pursue joy, you're going to have to be intentional about practicing gratitude and cultivating a heart of joy.

Next, intentionally and actively, pursue it and practice it, always intertwining it with gratitude. **Grateful** people are **joyful** people. The starting point? **Gratitude** for what Christ did for us on the cross.

The secret to cultivating a heart of **joy**? It's **gratitude.**

When we begin to notice, name, and nurture the blessings in our lives—big or small—we're cultivating a heart posture that invites **joy** to move in and stay awhile!

Still struggling to find your joy in the empty nest? Try making a list of what you've enjoyed about the empty nest so far. (Yes, even if it's only been a few days!) What are you grateful for? Use the space below to keep a running list and add to it every time you think of something new!

A joyful heart is good medicine, but a broken spirit dries up the bones.

Proverbs 17:22 (NASB)

I don't know about you, but for me, cultivating an attitude of gratitude and joy has been something that I've had to be very intentional about doing. I don't really think gratitude comes naturally to most of us, and developing a grateful heart in the empty nest has required thoughtfulness, intentionality, and faithfulness. The best thing? It has borne the fruit of joy in my life, which, in turn, makes my ongoing efforts to nurture gratitude well worth it! I think most of us tend to focus on life's annoyances and frustrations, but pursuing an attitude of gratitude is part of how we cultivate joy in our lives, and both are rooted in faith.

Throughout Scripture, we see that joy is intertwined with gratitude (see Psalm 126:3, Isaiah 9:3, 2 John 1:12). Grateful people are joyful people. They have gratitude for what Christ did for them on the cross and for the fact that he did it when we didn't deserve it. They recognize and are grateful for what he continues to do in their lives.

Let's break it down to the nitty gritty! If you're struggling with gratitude and joy right now, there are some practical things you can do to pursue it, nurture it, and lean into it. Remember, you have to *choose* joy. And then you have to keep choosing it— every single day!

> Pursuing an attitude of gratitude is part of how we cultivate joy in our lives, and both are rooted in faith.

1. Make an Effort to Laugh More (Especially at Yourself!):

It's important not to take ourselves too seriously.

2. Plan Something to Look Forward To:

My husband and I always try to have *something* fun to look forward to, whether it's a date night or a weekend getaway.

3. Sprinkle Positivity into Your Everyday Life:

Do little things like changing your passwords to something joyful and positive, like *gratefulgal21* or *ichoosejoy82*. Studies have found that small acts of affirmation actually activate the reward centers in our brains.[2]

4. Figure Out What Makes You "Happy":

Happiness, when intertwined with gratitude, can be a gateway to joy!

5. Create a Positivity Playlist:

It's no secret that music improves your mood! Look for an upbeat playlist on Spotify or compile a list of 10-20 songs to throw on when you need a little motivation.

6. Make an Effort to Smile More:

Studies have proven that there's a link between facial expression and mood.[3] When you smile, your brain releases neuropeptides, which combat stress. Other natural antidepressant neurotransmitters, such as dopamine, serotonin, and endorphins, are also activated. By making yourself smile, you're actually activating an area in the brain that's switched on when you're **joyful.** As Winston Churchill famously said, "Your day will go the way the corners of your mouth turn!"

7. Celebrate Everything:

Be sure you stop and celebrate with **gratitude** the

joyful events in life, big or small. Don't just go on to the next thing.

8. Worship:

Worship is acknowledging who God is and who we are, and then it's acknowledging that only He could bridge the divide between us. **Gratitude is always intertwined with joy**, which, in turn, is *always* intertwined with worship.

9. Guard Your Heart and Your Mind:

If we polled five people who know you well, would they describe you as a positive or a negative person? Would they say you have a heart of joy? Want to know if you have a heart of **joy**? Scripture provides us with a *failproof* test: What's coming out of your mouth? (Luke 6:45)

10. Actively Practice the Discipline of Gratitude:

Grateful people are joyful people.

If you want to cultivate a heart of joy, write down three things you're grateful for at the end of each day. Make them specific and unique to illuminate pockets of joy hidden throughout your day. Like, "My adult kid reached out to me to ask for advice." Avoid things that are repetitive or too general, like "I'm grateful for my family" or "I'm grateful for the beautiful weather." Be specific!

Power Prayers

"There is no greater influence
in your child's life than
your prayers for them."[4]

Stormie Omartian

When our children leave the nest, fear and anxiety can set in for us as parents. It did for me! Somehow, when they were home, I felt that I had some control. (As if!) But when they left home, any semblance of control I had was gone. And I became fearful. Fearful for their physical safety, fearful about their ability to make wise choices, and that their bad choices would have far-reaching consequences that might affect the rest of their lives.

Most of all, I feared that they wouldn't stay faithful to the Lord. The irony of this doesn't escape me! After all, 2 Timothy 1:7 tells us that *God did not give us a spirit of fear, but of power and of love and of a sound mind.*

Seriously, Suzy?

Like so many of us, my fear is rooted in a lack of faith,

and I know from Romans 10:17 that *"… faith comes by hearing, and hearing by the word of God"* (NKJV). Fear dissipates when I spend time in the Word, and when I pray *actual Bible verses* for my adult children. When I do that, **I know without a doubt that I'm aligning my prayers with the will of God.**

Here are some passages I pray for my adult children.

1. **Ephesians 1:17-19**: That the Lord would give them the **Spirit of wisdom and revelation of Him**, that **the eyes of their hearts would be opened** so that **they will know and cherish the hope to which He has called them; the riches of His glorious inheritance in the saints** (God's people); and what is **the immeasurable greatness of His power** in their lives, in accordance with the working of His mighty strength.

2. **Colossians 1:9-12**: I like this model of prayer from Paul! He prays specifically that those in the church at Colossae would be filled with the **knowledge of the Lord's will in all spiritual wisdom and understanding**. Why does he pray this? So that they will **walk in a manner worthy of the Lord, please**

him in all things, bearing fruit in every good work, and growing in their knowledge of him. He also prays that they would be **strengthened with all power, for endurance, and patience (with joy!)**. Finally, he prays that they would **give thanks to the Lord**, who was the one who qualified them to share in the inheritance of the saints.

3. **Philippians 4:19**: Our kids *will* be needy, and as empty nesters, we can't be there to meet their needs the way we could when they were younger. We must fully entrust them to the Lord. We want our kids to remember that **God will supply every need of theirs according to his riches in glory in Christ Jesus**.

4. **Micah 6:8**: This is our family verse! We want our children to remember that the Lord has told us what is good and what He requires of us: **to be just, to love kindness, and to walk humbly with our God**.

5. **Proverbs 4:23**: This world is a challenging place to be! We want our

kids to **guard their hearts diligently**. *Everything* we do and say flows out of our hearts (See Luke 6:45 and Proverbs 27:19).

6. **Hebrews 10:24**: We want our kids to be *leaders*, pointing others to faith. We pray that (through their words and their example) they would **encourage others to love and good deeds**.

Use the space below to write out one verse for
every day this week and commit to
pray it specifically for your kids.
Be sure to record His answers!

MONDAY

Answered Prayer

TUESDAY

Answered Prayer

WEDNESDAY

Answered Prayer

THURSDAY

Answered Prayer

FRIDAY

Answered Prayer

SATURDAY

Answered Prayer

SUNDAY

Answered Prayer

**In returning and rest you shall be
saved; in quietness and in trust shall
be your strength.**

Isaiah 30:15

You probably didn't realize how wound up you were
when the kids were in the nest. We didn't! But let's face
it, active and engaged high school kids tend to walk,
talk, and eat fast. When our kids left, we realized we
had been frantically trying to match their pace!

We noticed that when we went out to dinner, we
wolfed down our meals in ten minutes flat! We ate
quickly, talked quickly, and walked quickly. What had
happened to us?

Before the empty nest, many people dread the
quiet that comes when kids no longer live at home.
But so many empty nesters have told me that they
eventually come to cherish the peace and quiet. After

all, it's challenging to think when you're busy talking, answering questions, or helping *someone* with *something*!

In the quiet of the empty nest, I've rediscovered my love for music, gardening, and reading. Simply put, I can hear myself think. Now, we linger over meals and talk at length about our days during after-dinner walks in the neighborhood.

And can we talk about the privacy issue? *Lovely!* Right?

When our daughter, our last little bird to leave the nest, still lived at home, she had an uncanny knack for needing me *at the exact moment* I was naked. Every time! My husband joked that she must have some kind of "nudity radar" tracking system. We laughed so hard about it, we even coined our own word for it: "nadar" (you know, like *naked radar*). Hahaha!

To this day, that girl still somehow manages to FaceTime me *right* when I'm stepping out of the shower or in the middle of changing clothes. And yes, we still use "nadar" all the time! In fact, when I pick up her call now and I'm naked, I don't even say "Hi"—I just say, "Nadar!"

Ah, *exhale…*

How's your breathing? Are you eating, talking, or walking too fast? Use the space below to note the things you want to focus on doing more slowly this week. It's going to take a conscious effort to slow your pace and learn to savor the quiet and peacefulness of your empty nest.

Take Back the House

**Unless the Lord builds the house,
those who build it labor in vain.**

Psalm 127:1

When our nest emptied, we immediately called the painters, carpet cleaners, and floor refinishers to undo the years of damage our kids had inflicted on our home! In fact, it was all we could do to make ourselves wait until the last one left the nest to make repairs.

Once it was done, we felt like we were living in a brand-new house! Part of the joy of being an empty nester is that when you put something away, it stays there. When you clean something, it stays clean. When you make a bed, it stays made. The empty nest is kinda magical that way—and honestly, it felt like a little gift we'd been given after years of active parenting.

When we became empty nesters, we made the decision that we wouldn't downsize until our last child was out of college. We wanted our kids to have their familiar rooms to come home to during their school breaks. They appreciated that, and so did we—it made homecomings feel warm, welcoming, and just as they remembered.

But living in a big family home when it's just the two of you can be a lot to handle! We rattled around in there and felt like we were wasting money paying for space that we weren't really using anymore. The conversation about moving and downsizing was one we returned to several times a year after the kids left.

By the time we finally made the decision to downsize, we were truly ready to declutter and simplify our lives. Although going through years of memories was emotional at times, the thought of freeing up our finances, lightening our load, and creating space for new adventures was invigorating!

It gave us the energy and motivation we needed to get through the cleaning out phase—and believe me, that was no small feat!

Take a "tour" of your home like you're a guest seeing it for the first time. Make a list of three areas that could be simplified, repurposed, or cleared out. Then choose *one* small step to take this week. Clear a shelf, toss some clutter, or just start dreaming about what that space *could* become. Game room? Reading nook? Home Pilates studio? You're the boss now!

Simplify

Repurpose

Clear Out

I Choose You

In trying to explain marriage to our kids when they were young, we used a coin. We told them that the "heads" side of the coin represents a person's strengths, while the "tails" side represents their negative qualities. When you marry someone, you get the *whole* coin! There's no option to pick and choose the parts you like best—it's a package deal.

Over the years, my husband and I have come to realize that so many of the differences in the way we see and approach things are essentially a matter of temperament and personality type. And you know what? That's true in marriage, and it's true in parenting, too.

The truth is, we fall in love with a person's strengths— those wonderful, magnetic qualities that draw us to them. But it doesn't take long to realize we're also in a

relationship with their weaknesses! In fact, weaknesses
are often just strengths taken to an extreme, misapplied,
or showing up at the wrong time.

That's why it's so important to make the intentional
choice to reframe things—to focus on "heads" rather
than "tails" when it comes to the people we love. It's
a great word picture, no matter who you're dealing
with—spouse, friend, or especially, your adult kids.

The truth is, we fall in love
with a person's strengths—
those wonderful, magnetic
qualities that draw us to
them. But it doesn't take
long to realize we're also
in a relationship with their
weaknesses!

Let's be honest. When you're worried about your kids,
it's usually their weaknesses that come to mind first,
right? Those are the things that can keep you awake at
night! But here's the truth: You can't "fix" your adult
child. (Hard as you might try!) Only God can bring
about true and lasting change in their lives, just like He
does in ours.

But stop and break it down for a minute! Look again.
When you think about those weaknesses in your

children's lives, what are the corresponding strengths you see? These are the very qualities that, with time and maturity, will serve them well as they navigate life on their own.

Good job, mom! (See how we reframed that?!)

Use the lines below to write each child's name.
Write down those weaknesses that concern you.
Next to them, write the corresponding strength.

Freedom!

"Empty nesting is not about letting
go of your children; it's about
rediscovering yourself."[5]

Carin Rubenstein

Right before my nest emptied, I asked one of my friends (who was about a year into empty-nester life) what was different about her marriage now that the kids were gone. "Well, there's a lot more nudity!" she said. I think I screamed and put my hands over my ears in protest! Wow! Okay! Um ... I then proceeded to tell her that I was not looking for *that* kind of information! "No," she replied with a laugh, "what I mean is that when we're getting ready in the mornings, and we want something from the fridge, we just go and get it. No worries!"

At the time, I remember thinking that sounded fantastic, as well as a handy way to deal with hot flashes—just sayin'! I'm here to tell you that she was right. There is a lot of, um, *freedom* in the empty nest.

No one monitors your comings and goings. No one needs to know where you are going, what you're doing, and who is doing it with you! Since your schedule is no longer tied to a school schedule, *everything* is more convenient. It leaves room for flexibility and spontaneity!

If you have a flexible work schedule, take advantage of it and head out on a walk in the afternoon, or schedule a long lunch with an old friend. One day, I decided to take a bubble bath in the middle of the day—just to celebrate the fact that I could! Another day, I went to the movies by myself before noon and indulged in buttered popcorn and a large soda—just because I could!

It felt like a little celebration, and I reveled in the joy that I had the freedom to do it!

Can you think of little ways you can celebrate the freedom of the empty nest? Make a bucket list and get going!

FINDING YOUR PURPOSE IN THE EMPTY NEST

Purpose Beyond Parenthood

**The heart of man plans his way,
but the Lord establishes his steps.**

Proverbs 16:9

What does it mean to find your purpose? After the kids leave the nest, it can be challenging to figure out how life as an empty nester is supposed to look! It's a new season, full of freedom—but also full of questions.

Without a doubt, raising kids is a sacred calling. It's meaningful and rewarding work that grabs your heart, gives you purpose, and never really lets you go. You'll always be a parent. Don't forget that.

But with the kids gone, how will you spend your time? What will you do? How will you make a difference in the lives of others? And maybe even more importantly, what will fill *your* heart and bring *you* joy in this next chapter?

While it may sound kind of morbid, I thought a
lot about Psalm 90:12 when I became an empty
nester. That's the verse where the Lord reminds us to
number our days, that we may gain a heart of wisdom. I
remember thinking, "I guess I've got about a third of
my life left. How am I going to make it count?"

All the possibilities and choices about what's next can
be overwhelming and paralyzing. Where do you even
start? One thing I knew for sure: I wanted to keep
learning and growing in my empty-nester years. I
didn't want to just drift through them. Having a
systematic plan helped me break down what seemed
an impossible task into bite-sized pieces and made my
goals seem achievable.

More than anything, I wanted my kids to be proud of
me! I wanted to set an example of how to live the next
phase of life productively and with purpose. You can,
too! Just take it one step at a time. We're going to work
through it together.

What are the next steps you can take (like, tomorrow!)? Jot them down below. Don't overthink it—just start with one or two simple ideas that excite you or make you curious. Remember, small steps lead to big change over time. Consider this your invitation to dream a little, be brave, and take that very first step!

Pursue Your Passion(s)

> "If you can't figure out your purpose, figure out your passion. For your passion will lead you right into your purpose."[6]
>
> Bishop T.D. Jakes

Start by making a list of things you'd like to do that you might have put off in the child-rearing years. What gets your heart racing and your blood pumping? What do you love? What makes you excited? Do you want to travel? Go back to school? Enter or reenter the workforce? Start your own business? Become a volunteer extraordinaire or cultivate a hobby that you haven't had time for in the past eighteen-plus years? All of those are valid and meaningful!

Research how you could get more involved with what you love. We live in an era where information is just a keystroke away. It's a simple place to start.

Next, explore and learn more. Is there a group you can join, classes you can take, or an "expert" who would be willing to talk with you? Be brave and reach out to someone you admire in your area of interest! Chances are, they'll be flattered, honored, and excited to share their journey with you. Everyone loves to talk about themselves! I promise you'll find valuable advice. (And usually an offer for continued help!)

When I was trying to figure out my purpose in the empty nest, I talked to any and every empty nester I could find about how they spent their time! I even shadowed a few people who had jobs that were interesting to me.

As an empty nester, it can be tough to put yourself back into learning mode. After all, you're used to being the parent, the person in the know!

Humble yourself, be brave enough to ask for help, and expect that sometimes you may feel stupid and, well, kinda *old*. But you'll also learn that there are many people who are happy to help you and encourage you along the way.

Put some thoughts about how you could pursue your passions down on paper. Don't overthink it. Just jot down your initial ideas. Think of this as a brainstorming session! There are no ideas or thoughts too crazy.

Be Resourceful

"Do what you can, with what you
have, where you are."[7]

Theodore Roosevelt

Once you've narrowed down what you might like to
pursue, it's time to assess your resources.

Resources can be financial, of course, but they can also
be time, connections, knowledge, abilities, or even a
unique idea that sets you apart.

Don't sell yourself short! Chances are, you have more
resources than you realize—you've just been so busy
focusing on everyone else for so long that you haven't
taken stock of them in a while.

When I started my blog, Empty Nest Blessed, I spent
significant time checking out other blogs aimed
at empty nesters. I didn't find any other personal
blogs that had my specific take on the empty nest:
encouraging and resourcing women as they seek to
move forward with joy into the next stage of life. That
realization gave me confidence that there was a space

for my voice and my perspective. It helped me take that first (very scary!) step.

Whether you're taking on something big (like an entrepreneurial venture) or smaller (like a leadership position in an organization or volunteering in a new way), seek wise counsel from others who have walked the path (or a similar one) before you. Reach out to them. Ask questions. Most people are honored to share what they've learned—and their advice could save you time, money, or even heartache down the road. Plus, having someone cheering you on who's *been there* can be incredibly motivating.

As with most ventures, there may be startup costs when you begin. These may or may not be financial, but they *will* require an investment of some kind—whether it's time, energy, training, or other commitments. Take the time to investigate the potential cost before you begin, so there aren't any unwelcome surprises. Being resourceful means doing your homework, planning ahead, and setting yourself up for success!

Make a practical, detailed plan of the steps you need to take to achieve your goals. Get out a calendar and work on a realistic timetable. Assess your resources and include how you plan to seek wisdom and advice from others. Finally, share your plan with a mentor, family, and/or friends. There will come a time when you need a cheerleader or two to help you stay focused on your goals.

Don't You Dare Compare!

Are you paralyzed and afraid to start things for fear of embarrassment or even failure?

Don't wait to start until you get things perfect because if you do, you might never start! Remember, if something doesn't work, you can always change it later. Very, very few decisions in life are irreversible!

Try not to worry about what other empty nesters think, or what they're doing, or how they're coping. **Don't compare** what you do in a day, a week, a month, or a year to others. You may have restrictions or commitments that they don't have. Likewise, they may have resources available to them that you don't have.

As someone active on social media, I've learned

something important: When I *don't* share every detail of my life, people tend to fill in the blanks themselves—and their assumptions aren't always accurate! They create a version of me based on what I *do* share, but for everything I leave out? Their minds make up the rest. And often, that looks like putting me on a pedestal while unfairly downplaying themselves.

Here's the truth: When you see someone on social media (or anywhere else, really), you're only seeing what they *choose* to share. Nobody shows every messy moment, every struggle, or every insecurity. Remember that the next time you're tempted to compare your behind-the-scenes to someone else's carefully curated highlight reel!

> Don't compare what you do in a day, a week, a month, or a year to others.

Instead of comparing yourselves to others (or what you think you know about them), cultivate a humble heart, stay in your lane, and do things your way. No one has your unique set of gifts, abilities, and passions, and no one will do things exactly like you!

Find your specific niche, your unique take on things, or your one-of-a-kind viewpoint, and focus on embodying that fully and authentically. Stay true to yourself and keep your goal right in front of you. (Yes, like maybe even on a sticky note!)

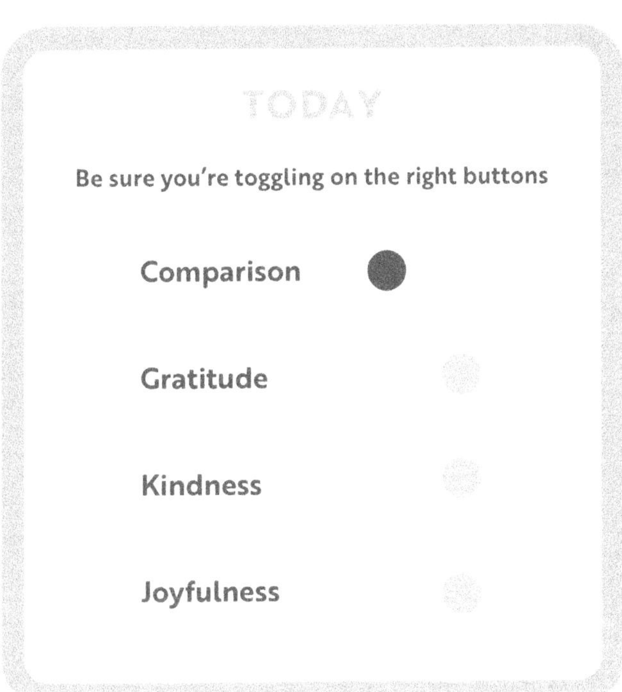

When I get discouraged, I always think about Matthew
4:1–11. For forty days and forty nights, Satan tempted
Jesus in the wilderness. Each time Satan tempted him,
Jesus responded with *truth*. Yep! He retorted with the
truth of Scripture. When you get discouraged, take
yourself back to Scripture and remind yourself of who
God says you are.

Armed with that reminder, get back on track.
Remember, you don't have to be perfect to be amazing!
You can do it! I believe in you.

What's holding you back? Do you think everything has to be perfect before you can take action? Are you trying to minimize or avoid the pain of judgment or failure? Is your identity wrapped up in where you see yourself in relation to others? There will always be people who are better than you at what you do, and there will always be people who are worse than you. *Action* is the antidote to these issues. Use the space below to make some plans!

Persevere

Let's face it! Most things are more difficult and time-consuming than they appear when you see the result. (This coming from the girl who, every time she watches figure skating, decides she can do a double axel. "That doesn't look too hard!")

But the truth is, if you want to find your purpose in the empty nest, it will probably mean sticking with something longer than you initially thought. Yep! You're going to need to persevere and stick with it. You're going to need to seek out people who will cheer you on and encourage you in your pursuit.

And guess what? You may even fail a little bit along the way. (Actually…you definitely *will!* I sure did!) But failure doesn't necessarily mean you're not on the right path—it usually just means you're learning and growing. Some of the best lessons come wrapped in challenges and setbacks.

One of my favorite books is *Grit: The Power of Passion & Perseverance* by Angela Duckworth. She believes that what truly drives success is not "genius" but a combination of passion and long-term perseverance, which she calls "grit." Her book inspired and motivated me as I sought to find my purpose in the empty nest. It reminded me that steady, faithful effort—even when nobody sees it—can lead to beautiful things.

> But failure doesn't necessarily mean you're not on the right path—it usually just means you're learning and growing.

The Bible has a lot to say about perseverance, too! Here are a few of the verses I cling to when I'm tempted to give up:

Galatians 6:9 — *And let us not grow weary of doing good, for in due season we will reap, if we do not give up.* (ESV)

James 1:2-4 — *Count it all joy, my brothers, when you meet trials of various kinds, for you know that the testing of your faith produces steadfastness.* (ESV)

Perseverance isn't about being perfect—it's about not quitting.

Choose one of the verses above that speaks to you and write it down below. As you write, say it out loud and begin to commit it to memory. Then post it somewhere you'll see it often—like your mirror or phone lock screen—as a reminder to keep going, even when things get tough.

For we are his workmanship, created in Christ Jesus for good works, which God prepared beforehand, that we should walk in them.

Ephesians 2:10

Your "work" is whatever you do that gives your life purpose and allows you to use your gifts and talents. In this season of life, that might look different for every empty nester! I have a friend who spends hours every day praying for others and preparing Bible study lessons to share with women in her church. That's her work. I have another friend who went back to school so she can take over her family's business when her parents are ready to retire. That's her work.

Others I know have obtained their real estate licenses, become volunteer museum docents, or started creative businesses, such as jewelry making, stationery design, or pottery. Each of them found meaningful work in the empty nest, but none of them got there overnight. It took time, perseverance, courage, and a whole lot of prayer.

But here's the most important thing to remember: Your worth is *not* in your work. Your identity is not found in what you accomplish, produce, or check off a to-do list. Your life has value and meaning simply because you were created by God and are deeply loved by Him.

When our daughter was little, she had an old, tattered lovey named Mimi. Mimi was smelly, worn, and more than a little ragged, but Becca adored her. When Becca went outside to play, she would lovingly hand Mimi to me for safekeeping. I never threw Mimi aside or stuffed her in a closet. I cared for her with great tenderness—not because of her appearance or usefulness, but because of how deeply she was loved by her owner.

Your life has value and
meaning simply because you
were created by God and are
deeply loved by Him.

And friend, that's exactly how God sees you. He cherishes you, not because of what you *do*, but because of who you *are*. Work hard to find your purpose in this season, but never forget: Your worth was settled long before your work began.

Where does your worth lie?
Be honest with yourself and write it down.
Then draw a big X over it and write down where
your worth is really found. (Hint: the verse at the
top of this section!)

LIFE
IN THE
EMPTY
NEST

Is This a
Good Time?

"Teach us to number our days, that
we may gain a heart of wisdom."

Psalm 90:12 (NIV)

Time is the greatest commodity we have, because it's the one thing we can never get back. Unlike money, possessions, or even energy, once time is spent, it's gone forever. We all have a finite amount of time, and we don't know how much we have, which makes it precious. You can earn more money, regain your health, and even rebuild broken relationships—but you can't create more time.

That's why it's worth thinking about the relationship you have with time. Are you chronically early because of anxiety? Maybe it's time to show yourself some grace and explore what's underneath that. Are you chronically late? I once had a friend tell me she cured her chronic lateness when she realized that by being late, she was "stealing" time, the most valuable thing her friend had.

She told me she'd never steal her friend's money or possessions, so once she reframed lateness that way, it changed everything.

When the kids were in the nest, their schedules provided structure for your schedule. From mealtimes to weekend schedules, time management was largely dictated by their activities and commitments. After all, you had to get people where they were going, on time, and with everything they needed! Even after the kids started driving, you were still managing mealtimes and a million other little things.

But with the kids out of the nest, you can be less *reactive* and more *proactive* about how you use your time. That's pretty exciting! But if you're like most of the empty nesters I talk to, becoming an empty nester probably does require some shifts in how you view and spend your time.

When you start thinking of time as your most valuable asset, you'll naturally become more mindful about how you use it, who you share it with, and what you invest it in. (And that's a good thing!)

Are you stressed about how to use the extra time you have as an empty nester? I have a friend whose anxiety is so triggered by time she doesn't even wear a watch!

Jot down your thoughts about time. What concerns you as an empty nester?

Nobody Told Me!

Behold, I am doing a new thing; now it springs forth, do you not perceive it? I will make a way in the wilderness and rivers in the desert.

Isaiah 43:19

I'm just going to give it to you straight. There are a few things about the empty nest that no one talks about. Oh, you probably expected the sadness. And you probably figured you'd feel some degree of uncertainty about the future. But there are some things nobody warns you about—little things that can sneak up on you and catch you off guard. We're getting real, y'all... but we're also going to find joy in the realness.

1. The adjustment may take longer than you thought.

There is no "normal" time frame for adjusting to the empty nest. Transitioning to this new season often involves grief, and grief is a deeply personal experience. There's no timetable! Give yourself grace. Be patient with yourself. And if you feel stuck in your grief, consider reaching out for help. Many people do, and it can be a healthy step toward healing.

2. You're going to think about your kids more than they think about you.

It's not that they don't love you—of course they do! It's just that love, like water, flows most naturally from the top down. Rather than dwelling on how often they think of you, shift your focus: Look for the little ways your influence still shows up in their lives. If you look, you'll see it in their habits, their values, and even their speech. It's there. I promise!

3. You may feel jealous of your kids.

They're young, they're gorgeous, and it seems like their whole lives are in front of them. And you? Well, you may feel old, tired, and a little discouraged. No one wants to admit they feel this way, but in my experience, it's fairly common. The good news? This season is full of opportunities for *you,* too!

4. You'll miss the little, everyday moments the most.

It's not just the significant milestones that may make

you tear up. It's the empty pantry that used to be raided, the quiet mornings without the school rush, and the way the house stays just a little *too* clean.

5. You may feel guilty for feeling free and happy.

Please don't! It doesn't mean you love them any less. Be grateful for this exciting new season. Then go out and do something you love—with joy and without apology!

Do you relate to any of those? Be honest. Use the space below to jot down what's surprised you about the empty nest.

**Then he said to them, 'Watch out!
Be on your guard against all kinds
of greed; life does not consist in an
abundance of possessions.'**

Luke 12:15 (NIV)

Whether you're planning to downsize or not, when the kids move out, it's a natural time to declutter, clean out, and take stock. Even if you're staying right where you are, you can still "downsize" the number of your belongings and create more breathing room in your home (and maybe even in your heart!).

Getting started can often be the most challenging part! Our homes—and all the things inside them—hold memories. Some are sweet, some are bittersweet, and yes, some may bring a few tears. (I shed plenty!) But those tears are evidence of a life well-lived and well-loved. Expect them, embrace them, and let them remind you how blessed you've been.

These tips (from one who's done it) can help.

1. **Investigate ways to save memories digitally,** like photos, videos, kids' art work, or old home movies. It's a wonderful way to preserve them without taking up physical space.

2. **Let your kids know you're decluttering** and ask what they'd like to have. You might be surprised at what's meaningful to them!

3. **Consider making a keepsake box for each child**, filled with the treasures you've lovingly saved through the years.

4. **Ask for help!** A trusted friend or family member can help you stay on task (and keep you from getting stuck reminiscing over every item).

5. **Create a plan and a flexible schedule** to avoid feeling overwhelmed.

6. **Tackle one room at a time**, moving clockwise around the room to stay focused.

7. **Keep only what is useful, beautiful, or sparks joy**.

8. **Don't hang onto things** out of guilt, obligation, or "someday" thinking.

9. **If you're moving, know your new space** and measurements. Not sure about a piece? Bring it! If it doesn't work, you can always bless someone else with it.

Having trouble getting started? Try tackling one drawer, like your makeup drawer or the junk drawer. The great feeling you have when you're finished with even one drawer will motivate you to continue.

"A successful marriage requires
falling in love many times, always
with the same person."[10]

Mignon McLaughlin

How's your empty-nester marriage?

If you're married, you'll probably notice the dynamics
in your marriage shifting when your nest empties.
That's normal! Some empty nesters have told me their
first months felt like a second honeymoon! One of my
friends told me that she and her husband had started
flirting again, and they loved having the freedom to go
on dates whenever they wanted.

On the other hand, some couples find that they've
grown apart after years of focusing on their children
instead of their marriage. Others may have spent years
building their careers instead of prioritizing family. For
some, there's infidelity. For others, it's just a slow drift
apart into living separate lives.

Whatever the state of your union, that empty-nester marriage of yours could probably use some nurturing!

I remember falling in love with my husband all over again when I watched him step into fatherhood. There was something so special about seeing him love, lead, and nurture our kids. But what surprised me was that it happened again in the empty nest. Just like I had grown and changed through the years of raising our family, so had he. And when the noise and busyness of parenting quieted, I finally had the time and space to really see the man he had become.

It made me fall for him all over again—in a whole new way. With fewer distractions and more time to focus on each other, we rediscovered our connection, shared new experiences, and deepened our love in ways I never expected.

Whatever the state of your union, that empty-nester marriage of yours could probably use some nurturing!

Does your marriage need a little attention? Here are a few practical things that you can begin to work on today:

1. **<u>Make eye contact</u>**: How often do you look your husband in the eyes for more than a split second? Eye contact builds intimacy!

2. **<u>Laugh more</u>**: Life is too short to take *everything* so seriously! Find shared things to laugh about and get your giggle on.

3. **<u>Flirt</u>**: One day, when my husband left his phone on the counter, I opened it and went to my page on his contacts app. Once there, I changed my name from "Suzy" to "My Hot Wife." The next time I called him, he answered the phone laughing so hard he could barely breathe!

4. **<u>Smile more</u>**: People who smile are perceived as more attractive, likable, and competent. Not to mention, smiling stimulates the release of neurotransmitters, like dopamine and serotonin, which are associated with feelings of pleasure and happiness.

5. **<u>Say "Thank you"</u>**: Those two little words can transform your empty-nester

marriage. Try looking for more things to thank your spouse for! You'll see him in a whole new light!

6. **<u>Hug it out</u>**: Hugs release oxytocin, which is responsible for that warm, loving feeling we get when we give or receive a hug.

Make a list of at least three things you're going
to do today to strengthen your marriage, then
do them! (I highly recommend #3 above!)

1.

2.

3.

Dating, Empty-Nester Style

"A marriage is like a garden—if you don't water it, the flowers stop blooming."[11]

Chuck Swindoll

When your nest is empty, every night is a potential date night! Whether you're married or single, the possibility is out there! (And that's something to celebrate!)

If you're married, sometimes it's great to stay home and revel in the slower pace and the sweet quiet of just hanging out together. I love it when my husband and I are both home, and I'm doing my thing in one room, and he's doing his thing in another. It just feels easy and *companionable*. But as cozy as that is, we don't want to get stuck in that same routine night after night! Keeping things fresh and fun takes a little effort, but it's so worth it!

If you're single and dating, know that you have a big

advantage as an empty nester—you know yourself better than ever. You've gained life experience, resilience, and especially clarity about what truly matters in a partner. You're not trying to build a life from scratch—you're just looking for someone to complement the life you already have.

Whatever your relationship status, the key is not falling into the same old dinner-and-a-movie rut (unless, of course, that's what you both love!). Are there new hobbies, interests, or adventures you've always wanted to try? Pickleball is wildly popular with empty nesters—but so are things like taking cooking classes, visiting a farmer's market, enjoying live music, or even exploring new parts of your own hometown. When was the last time you packed a picnic or wandered through a local museum?

Whatever you choose to do, look for things that get you out of your routine, help you share new experiences, and (best of all) give you plenty of reasons to laugh together.

If you're married, plan a surprise date night for your spouse tonight! If you're single, grab some friends or ask someone you've been dying to get to know better to join you for an adventure.

50 Great Date Night Ideas for Empty Nesters

1. Take a picnic to a park you've never visited.

2. Visit the local farmer's market.

3. Visit the grocery store and gather all your favorite ingredients for DIY ice cream sundaes.

4. Go to a bookstore and browse the travel section.

5. Go out for ice cream.

6. Recreate your first date.

7. Go to the zoo.

8. Fly a kite.

9. Go fruit picking at a local farm.

10. Take a walking or biking tour of your city.

11. Get up early and watch the sunrise, then go out to breakfast.

12. Go for a walk and hold hands the whole time.

13. Go "catch-and-release" fishing.

14. Take $20 to the Dollar Store and spend it on crazy stuff.

15. Rent a tandem bike and go for a ride.

16. Go to a local tourist spot you've never visited.

17. Hit the batting cages.

18. Play frisbee golf.

19. Paint your own pottery.

20. Go to an arboretum or botanical garden.

21. Watch your wedding video.

22. Go bowling.

23. Get a couples massage.

24. Do a puzzle.

25. Play a board game.

26. Make s'mores in the fireplace.

27. Put down a waterproof mat and have a picnic in your bed.

28. Play "20 Questions."

29. Make a "bucket list" of places you want to go and things to do.

30. Have a dance party in the living room.

31. Make homemade pizzas.

32. Bake cookies from scratch and eat them warm from the oven.

33. Host a game night with friends.

34. Go thrift store shopping and buy each other something. ($20 spending limit!)

35. Take a dance class.

36. Go ice skating or roller skating.

37. Play putt-putt.

38. Watch the sunset.

39. Paint-by-number.

40. Try a new coffee shop.

41. Have a spa day.

42. Visit a museum.

43. Go hiking.

44. Rent a tandem bike.

45. Make a music playlist together.

46. Go to a concert or live theater.

47. Make breakfast for dinner.

48. Have a fondue night.

49. Buy some plants at the nursery and get planting!

50. Learn to roll sushi.

Cooking for Two

He makes grass grow for the cattle,
and plants for people to cultivate—
bringing forth food from the earth:
wine that gladdens human hearts,
oil to make their faces shine, and
bread that sustains their hearts.

Psalm 104:14–15 (NIV)

Learning to cook in the empty nest is an adjustment!
(And, based on the empty-nester moms I talk to, one
that catches a lot of people by surprise!)

Without the chaos of teenagers rushing in and out and
trying to adjust mealtimes to their crazy schedules,
many empty nesters find that they enjoy cooking again.
I've never loved to cook, but as an empty nester, I've
actually learned to find cooking *relaxing*!

However, shifting your recipes to smaller portions can
be a significant adjustment. Cooking for two (or one)

is *not* the same as cooking for a family! And you don't want to end up throwing out a bunch of food or having to store lots of leftovers.

One of my favorite things about the empty nest is not having to worry about matching my menu selections to the preferences of a family of five. (I love you, kids, but it was hard to cook for all of you at once!) With just the two of us now, we can eat what *we* want. Truthfully, we eat lighter and healthier as empty nesters!

I can remember heading to the grocery store for the first time after our nest emptied. It was a revelation! Suddenly, shopping was faster, simpler, and surprisingly budget-friendly. I remember feeling downright giddy when I realized this once-dreaded chore might become—dare I say—*enjoyable* in the empty nest!

Now, maybe some of you are total foodies. Perhaps you enjoy watching cooking shows or happily read cookbooks as if they were novels. (I love that for you, but I'm just *not* that girl!) But I *will* say this: cooking for just the two of us has made me a *little* more adventurous in the kitchen.

One fun surprise? I've actually rediscovered my slow cooker! (I know ... "adventurous" and "slow cooker" don't usually go hand in hand, but hear me out!) Back when the kids were home, I used my giant slow cooker all the time, cranking out big batches of chili, hearty stews, or pot roast for a hungry crew. But these days? I've downsized, and I'm loving it. I picked up a two-quart slow cooker, and it's just the right size for two. Perfect for cozy meals without a week's worth of leftovers!

How can you adapt your favorite recipes for the empty nest? I'm sharing a few of our favorite recipes-for-two (they work great for one also)!

Chimichurri Sauce

This easy sauce is healthy and will spice up any kind of
grilled meat you can think of. (But I like it on chicken
or flank steak the best.) Let's get cooking—or food
processing—to be more accurate!

Chimichurri is pronounced chee-mee-CHOO-ree,
which might just be the most *fabulous* word to say! You
can go ahead and roll those Rs, because it originated
in Argentina! It is typically made with parsley, minced
garlic, oregano, and white vinegar. Later, Uruguay
added red pepper flakes for an additional kick.

My chimichurri sauce recipe is very traditional and
takes only about 5 minutes to prepare. I use Italian
parsley (also known as flat-leaf parsley). It has more
serrated leaves than its ruffled cousin, curly-leaf
parsley, and it has a stronger flavor with a clean, slightly
peppery taste.

Some people have compared chimichurri to pesto
because they look kind of similar. It's not pesto! Pesto is
made from basil, olive oil, garlic, nuts, and cheese, and
it's used with pasta. Chimichurri, on the other hand,

is made from oil, water, vinegar, parsley, and assorted herbs and spices, and it's used with meats.

- 1 cup firmly packed fresh Italian parsley leaves

- 3-4 cloves garlic (I use pre-chopped.)

- 2 Tbsp. fresh oregano leaves (or 2 tsp. dried oregano)

- 1/3 cup extra virgin olive oil

- 2 Tbsp. distilled white vinegar (or red or white wine vinegar, if you prefer)

- 1/2 tsp. salt

- 1/8 tsp. black pepper

- 1/4 tsp. red pepper flakes

Place the parsley, oregano, and garlic into a small food processor. Place into a small bowl and stir in the olive oil, vinegar, salt, pepper, and red pepper flakes. Adjust the seasonings to your taste.

Serve immediately or refrigerate. It can be stored for a week or two.

Mexican Chicken

The best thing about this chicken recipe is that it is seasoned with cumin and topped with cilantro. Cumin contains a heart-healthy antioxidant called curcumin that is high in iron and aids in digestion. It adds flavor to food and contains only 10 milligrams of sodium. Cilantro (aka coriander) is one of those herbs that people seem to either love or hate. (I have a friend who swears it tastes like *soap*!) I happen to love it! It's a source of fiber, full of antioxidants, and beneficial to digestion. If it's not your favorite, don't worry. It's just a topping on this dish; you can leave it off if you prefer.

This recipe serves four. That means you can eat half now and freeze the remainder, or (even better), invite a couple of empty-nester pals over and enjoy a fun night together!

- Cooking spray

- 4 skinless, boneless chicken breast halves

- 3/4 tsp. ground cumin, divided use

- 1/4 tsp. salt

- 1 (10-oz.) can diced tomatoes and green chiles, undrained

- 3/4 cup shredded reduced-fat Mexican blend cheese

- 2 Tbsp. chopped cilantro

Coat a large skillet with cooking spray. Sprinkle both sides of chicken with 1/2 tsp. cumin and salt; cook 6 minutes over medium-high heat or until done. Remove chicken from pan and keep warm. Add 1/4 tsp. cumin and tomatoes to pan and cook 1 minute. Return the chicken to the pan and spoon tomato mixture over. Top with cheese, remove from heat, and cover for 1-2 minutes until cheese is melted. Top with cilantro if desired.

Layered Salad for Two

- 1 cup cooked, cooled quinoa

- 1 cup arugula lettuce, ready to eat

- 1 cup radicchio lettuce, ready to eat

- 1 avocado, diced into small cubes

- 1 Tbsp. lemon juice

- 12 red mini-cherub tomatoes, sliced in half lengthwise

- 2 chicken breasts, cooked, diced, and cooled

- 1 cup iceberg lettuce

- 8 asparagus spears, trimmed and steamed for about 1 minute

- 4 yellow mini-cherub tomatoes, sliced in half lengthwise

- Salt & pepper to taste

- Your favorite salad dressing

On the bottom of a bowl, spoon the quinoa, then layer the arugula and radicchio on top, in that order. Toss the diced avocado in the lemon juice and place it on top of the radicchio. Continue layering in the order listed above, with the red tomatoes, diced chicken breast, and the iceberg lettuce. Add the asparagus spears and yellow tomatoes on top.

Serve. Each person can season to taste and add salad dressing.

Sweet Summer Salad

As the weather heats up, a great summer salad seems like the perfect dinner! This one is super simple, quick, and refreshing. We eat it once a week in the warmer months!

- Arugula lettuce (I use organic, pre-packaged.)

- Crumbled goat cheese

- Berries of your choice

- Roasted pecan halves (optional)

- Cooked, cubed chicken breast (optional)

- Balsamic dressing (use your favorite brand or mix 1/4 cup olive oil, 1/2 cup balsamic vinegar, and 1 packet stevia)

Mix dressing well. Wash berries and let dry in a colander. Toss salad and dress to taste. Enjoy!

Maximize Your Minutes

"The bad news is time flies. The good news is you're the pilot."[12]

Michael Altshuler

In the beginning, finding structure and accomplishing the things you want to do in your empty nest can be more of a challenge than you thought! The truth is, we tend to fill up the time we have.

Have you ever heard of "Parkinson's Law"? It's the adage that work expands to fill the time allotted for its completion. The term was first coined in 1955 by Cyril Northcote Parkinson. He wrote a humorous essay for *The Economist* in which he shared the story of a woman whose only task in a day is to send a postcard. Sounds quick and easy, right? But her day fills quickly! She spends an hour thoughtfully selecting the perfect card (scenic landscape or floral print?), then another thirty minutes searching for her glasses (which she eventually finds on top of her head!). She takes ninety minutes to write the message, pausing often to consider what details to include, rewording a sentence, or reminiscing about the recipient. Then she prepares to walk to the mailbox. She deliberates for twenty minutes over whether to bring an umbrella, checks the forecast, changes her shoes, and looks for a jacket. At last, she mails the postcard—just before dinnertime. What should have taken five minutes has somehow filled her entire day!

Parkinson's point? It's not the difficulty of the job that determines how long it takes—it's the time we allow for it. And sometimes, the more time we have, the more we find to do.

If you're struggling to manage your time in the empty nest, try these tips:

1. **Embrace Your Natural Tendencies:**
   Don't try to be who you're not! If you like routine, stick with it, even if others say it's boring. If you need variety, build that into your day.

2. **Focus on Good Decision Making:**
   Most decisions aren't black or white, and most are reversible! Stressed about making the "wrong" decision? Try telling yourself that __________ is the

best decision "right now," but you can probably change your mind if circumstances change.

3. **Remember the HALT Acronym:** Don't make decisions when you're Hungry, Angry, Lonely, or Tired.

4. **Use Good Tools:** Remember that planners and schedules are just tools! Real life will always look different. Build margin into your day.

5. **Finish Strong:** Only take on commitments if you know that you can see them through to the end.

6. **Live Your Purpose:** You can't do it all, and you can't be everything to everyone! Narrow your focus, refine your purpose, and concentrate where you can thrive and make a difference.

As we've already established, the key to joy in the empty nest is to find the intersection between your passion and your skills so you can make a difference in the lives of others. Rank the six points above from 1 to 6 in order of what you're doing well to what you need to work on doing better.

1.

2.

3.

4.

5.

6.

Priority Pivot, Pivotttt, Pivottttt

"The key is not to prioritize what's on your schedule, but to schedule your priorities."[13]

Stephen R. Covey

How have your priorities shifted since your kids left the nest?

Are you living out your priorities? Do you need a priority pivot?

When it comes to managing your time, laying out your basic life priorities is a critical exercise in making good time management decisions.

For me, they lay out something like this:

1. My faith

2. My husband

3. My kids, their spouses, and my
   grandkids

4. My parents and extended family

5. My health and wellness

6. Work

7. My friends

8. Our home and belongings

Use the space below to write out your basic life
priorities.

Of course, there are times when these priorities will shift! Are your aging parents moving? Do you have an adult child who just had a baby and needs your help? Are you facing a health crisis? For a time, those things will alter the priorities on your list. That's as it should be!

Now, go deeper. Does the way you spend your time every day reflect your priorities? What does this look like?

This is what it looks like for me:

1. Reading the Bible and praying.

2. Caring for my relationships. (Answering texts from my kids, taking flowers to a sick friend, etc.)

3. Exercising and taking care of my health.

4. Work.

5. Running our household (making sure there's food in the house and I have a meal plan, keeping our home clean and organized, working on whatever house project we have going at the moment, etc).

Make a list of how you're going to live out your priorities daily. Your list won't look exactly like mine, and it may shift throughout the days, weeks, or months, and that's okay. But think through it and get it down on paper.

Dollars & Sense in the Empty Nest

She considers a field and buys it;
with the fruit of her hands she plants
a vineyard. She dresses herself with
strength and makes her arms strong.
She perceives that her merchandise is
profitable. Her lamp does not go out
at night.

Proverbs 31:16–18

With more time on your hands in the empty nest, contributing to your family's financial bottom line by generating income becomes a real possibility! Whether you just want to make some "fun money" or you need to help finance your kids' higher education, here are some ideas that can help you make some (possibly significant) money.

1. **Clean Out and Consign**: Becoming an empty nester is the perfect time to clean out those closets and consign your old clothes.

2. **Sell Your Old Electronic Devices**: Look online for sites that purchase used devices. Be sure to restore your device to its factory settings (thus removing all your private information) before selling it.

3. **Trade in Unused Gift Cards**: If you have gift cards you aren't going to use, you can get cash or trade them in for gift cards you *will* use. Search online for sites that purchase them.

4. **Become a Virtual Assistant**: A virtual assistant is an independent (typically home-based) professional who supports a business by assisting with administrative tasks, business development, social media management, graphic design, marketing, or other activities.

5. **Start a Small Business**: Interested in something more permanent, like a

full or part-time job? Do you have a
passion, hobby, or skill that would make
you a successful entrepreneur?

6. **Tutor or Teach**: Look into tutoring
services or teach classes or workshops in
a skill you excel in. One of my friends
taught after-school cooking classes in
her home to groups of five elementary
students at a time! It was a great idea
and a huge success!

7. **Freelance**: Pursue freelance work in
writing, design, photography, graphic
design, or other creative fields.

8. **Become a Consultant**: Offer consulting
services in an area of expertise.

9. **Love Animals?**: Offer pet-sitting or
dog-walking services in your local area.

10. **Invest**: Invest in stocks, real estate, or
other passive income streams.

11. **Become a Tour Guide**: If you're
especially knowledgeable about your
area, investigate local opportunities.

How can you leverage your extra time
in the empty nest to generate income?
Use the space below to jot down a
few ideas. Then jump in and get busy.

Making Friends at Midlife

> "Friendship is born at that moment
> when one person says to another,
> 'What! You too? I thought I was the
> only one.'"[14]
>
> C.S. Lewis

When I talk to empty nesters, they tell me that one of the biggest surprises of the empty nest was realizing just how much of their social life revolved around their kids.

Think about it! The parents you chatted with at soccer games, PTA meetings, and school events were a built-in community, but now that the kids are gone, those friendships may naturally fade. And honestly? That can feel a little lonely.

Longing for deeper connections in this new season? You're not alone. And here's the good news: Midlife can be an excellent time to make meaningful, lasting friendships! The beauty of midlife friendships is that they're built on *choice,* not just *circumstance.* You get to choose your friends based on who *you* are, not just who your kids were friends with or what activities they were part of. How great is that?

Ready to make new friends? Start by putting yourself in places where friendships can naturally grow! Have you always wanted to learn to play pickleball? Join a beginner's league. Love reading? A book club might be a perfect fit. Ready to go deeper in your faith? Join a Bible study at your church or in your community.

Think fitness classes, art workshops, hiking groups, or a cooking class—all these can be the perfect setting to find like-minded people who share your interests. Have a heart for serving others? Volunteering is a wonderful way to meet kindred spirits while making a difference in the lives of others.

Taking the first step can feel a little scary and intimidating—I get it! But remember, so many people are in the same boat, hoping for connection just like you.

Be brave and be the one who initiates!

Start with something simple: introduce yourself, ask a question, or suggest grabbing coffee after a class. Little gestures often lead to big friendships. And in this season of life? Those just might be the sweetest friendships of all.

Make a list of *three* activities or interests you'd love to explore but haven't yet. Now, do a little research and select *one* group, class, or event where you can meet new people. Then, take the leap! Sign up today, introduce yourself to someone new, and make that new friend.

1.

2.

3.

How to Get Your Groove Back

Though my flesh and my heart fail,
God is the rock of my heart, my
portion forever.

Psalm 73:26 (TLV)

Make no mistake, mama. You're in a significant life transition. If you're struggling to get your groove back, it's okay. I've talked to moms who feel like they still don't have their feet under them—even months or *years* into the empty nest. If that's you, be kind to yourself.

Now let's take inventory and help you get your groove back!

1. Check Your Emotional, Spiritual, and Mental Health

- Are you spending time in God's Word and in prayer every day? (This is first in this list for a reason—it's the most important!)

- Are you exercising regularly? (Thanks
  to endorphins, exercise can help with
  mental health.)

- Are you making good food choices?

- Are you getting enough sleep?

- Are you getting out of the house and
  spending time with others?

2. Schedule a Checkup: Schedule an appointment with your gynecologist for a thorough check-up. This is the season of life when hormones can go a little crazy! Anxiety and its evil cousin, depression, are pervasive during this time. There's *nothing wrong* with getting help! *Believe me*, what you are experiencing is very common, and your doctor will have heard it before—probably many times!

3. Watch Your Neediness: Being overly needy or demanding will push your kids away. You're adjusting to a new stage in life; they are, too. You *must* be the grownup! Don't place the burden of *your* empty nest adjustment on your kids. For your relationship with your kids to continue growing, make sure you're a positive and encouraging person in your child's life.

4. Stop Being Worried About What Others Are Doing or Thinking: Are you *really* worried about what other people think of you… or could it be that deep down, it's really about what *you* think of you, and you're just using "other people" as the excuse? Something to ponder!

5. Give Yourself Away: Prolonged grief, anxiety, and depression are inward-looking and self-focused. Consider how you can serve others. Even if you don't feel like it right now, know that you have so much to share! God can use you powerfully in the lives of others.

Take control back. You're not a victim, and only you can take action to improve your situation. This can be as small as getting out of bed and going to the gym, or it could be as big as working up the courage to go back to school. You were a role model for your kids all their lives. Don't stop now!

Me Time— It's Okay!

"This is your time. No guilt, no apologies, just you stepping into who you were meant to be."[15]

Mel Robbins

When I talk to empty nesters, many tell me they struggle to give themselves permission to focus on themselves after their kids leave the nest. Motherhood is about putting others first, and you've already raised *actual human beings*. That's amazing! It's time to celebrate that, and it's time to give yourself a little "me" time. I *officially* give you permission!

Begin by prioritizing your health and fitness. Most of us know what to do; we just need to do it. If you need to visit your physician, a nutritionist, or a personal trainer to get started, do it! You want to be healthy and strong for all the good times to come. (From graduations and weddings to grandkids!)

Even though you know that beauty goes *way* beyond the external, your appearance (and especially *how you feel about it*) is an important part of who you are. While none of us wants to be *defined* by our appearance, it's okay to give attention to the way we look!

Visit your dermatologist and talk honestly about the skin and beauty issues that are bugging you. From over-the-counter lotions and potions all the way up to in-office beauty procedures, there's a lot you can do to help you feel more confident in your skin. (Literally!)

If you don't have a clue what's in style or how to dress your midlife body, you're not alone. (I hear that a lot!) Don't worry! There are lots of places to turn for help. Ask a fashionable friend where she shops, or find some stylish influencer on social media (like me!) to follow for advice and recommendations. Or schedule a styling appointment at a place like Talbots, Anthropologie, or Nordstrom to receive free one-on-one help from a professional stylist.

Get busy! What next steps do you need to take to feel better about yourself? It's your turn, and remember, I gave you permission! Use the space below to make a to-do list.

Aging with Attitude (and Gratitude!)

Wisdom is with the aged, and understanding in length of days.

Job 12:12 (NASB)

If becoming an empty nester has you suddenly contemplating aging, you're not alone! Some days I love getting older, and some days I don't. I think that's normal!

Dealing with aging parents, wayward kids, health struggles, or financial woes can be challenging and difficult, but we can *choose* to look at the blessings and joys of aging, even in the midst of struggles. Once the kids left, I began keeping a gratitude journal, focusing on both large and small things that brought me joy every day. Eventually, I found myself recognizing things I was thankful for, and I realized I didn't need to wait until I could jot them down in my journal! Instead, I paused to thank God for them at that moment.

Like so much in life, it's *all* about the way you look at it. Let's *choose* to look at it with joy and gratitude! I hope you'll live life fully, no matter your age!

Here are ten reasons to love getting older and embrace aging:

1. **You care (a lot) less what others think**: If the teenage years are the apex of peer pressure, the post-fifty years are the polar opposite of that!

2. **You can keep learning and growing**: Satisfy your curiosity by traveling, joining a book club, taking a class, or learning a new language.

3. **You have the perspective of time**: You're not as afraid of making mistakes or making the "wrong" decision. Every decision isn't life or death, and the difference between right and wrong isn't always black and white.

4. **You have a greater sense of contentment**: You're grateful for all your blessings, whatever your present circumstances.

5. **You can take advantage of opportunities that come your way**: Opportunities abound to serve others, make a difference in the world, and share your wisdom and experience with those who need inspiration.

6. **You appreciate the slowness and quiet**: In the quiet, you can hear your own thoughts.

7. **You have a stronger sense of self**: You know yourself better, and you're more accepting *of* and confident *with* who you are.

8. **You have a sense of urgency**: You understand that the days are long, but the years are short, and you're more focused on making a difference and leaving a legacy.

9. **You can devote more time to important relationships**: You have a deeper understanding and appreciation of the value of relationships.

10. **You have a better handle on your purpose.**

How are you feeling about aging? Use the space below to jot down five struggles you're having and five things you've come to appreciate about getting older.

PARENTING ADULT KIDS

Parenting Adult Children (Sorta)

You don't really "parent" adult children. At least not in the way you've been parenting. Parenting children involves correcting, instructing, teaching, and training, as well as encouraging and supporting them.

But when it comes to parenting adult children, it's a completely different dynamic.

If you continue to parent adult children the way you always have—correcting, instructing, teaching, training, or even just "advising" and "suggesting"—you may (*and I don't say this lightly*) **lose** your relationship with your adult child.

One of the biggest challenges you'll face as a parent is making the transition from parenting your young children to establishing a healthy, adult-to-adult relationship with your grown kids. But shift you must—for the sake of your relationship and for their independence.

Here's why this is tricky: You really don't *parent* adult kids in the traditional sense anymore. But... (and this is *big*) if you work to cultivate your relationship, you may win their hearts as a coveted encourager, a trusted advisor, and a faithful friend.

So, how do you build a strong relationship with your adult children?

1. **Remember Who You're Dealing With** – Your kids think differently than you do because they're from a different generation. Get familiar with the characteristics of their generation as opposed to your own, so you can understand them better.

2. **Stay in Contact Using "Little Touches"** – Send them intermittent texts of things like Bible verses, online videos they'd find amusing, and information on topics of shared interest. (My husband and sons text through every Dallas Cowboys football game!)

3. **Keep Your Eyes on the Prize** – Your goal is to have a meaningful adult relationship with your grown kids. Think about the other meaningful relationships in your life and take some time to think objectively about what it looks like to be a good friend.

4. **Ask for Help** – *Tell* your kids that you're working at learning to be a good parent and friend to them as adults. (Your humility will mean a lot to them.) Give them permission to let you know when you've overstepped.

5. **Get Them Alone** – It's fun to have all your kids together and observe their adult sibling interactions, but if you really want to build your relationship with them as individuals, you need to spend time with each of them alone.

Stop right now and send one of those "little touches" to your kids. Tell them how you're praying for them. Ask them how their big project turned out. Or send them a funny video that will make them laugh. Do it!

How to Be the Parent They Want to Talk To

Set a guard, O LORD, over my mouth; keep watch over the door of my lips!

Psalm 141:3

Are you a good conversationalist? Or do you unintentionally hijack a conversation? Do you "**shift**" or do you "**support**" in conversation?

Picture this: Your son tells you about a stressful work situation, and before you know it, you're telling him about a similar experience you had twenty years ago. Or your daughter shares her excitement about an upcoming trip, and suddenly you're telling her about your own travels to the same spot.

Yikes! We've all been there!

While your *intent* may be to build intimacy by showing that you share common ground, when you **shift** a conversation onto yourself, you've *actually* commandeered the conversation and pulled the focus away from your child. Instead of feeling **supported**, they may feel unheard or marginalized.

By keeping the focus on *them* by using **supportive responses rather than shifting responses**, we demonstrate that we value who they are and how they feel. That's the kind of love and support they'll want to keep coming back for.

So, how do we keep the conversation about *them*? Here are a few tips:

1. **Mirror, Don't Magnify**: When they share something, reflect their feelings instead of adding your own. If they say, *"I'm nervous about my new job,"* instead of responding with, *"Oh, I remember when I started my first job…"* say something like, *"That makes so much sense! What's the part you're most concerned about?"*

2. **Ask, Don't Assume**: Instead of offering advice right away, ask open-ended questions like, *"What do you think you'll do?"* or *"How are you feeling about*

that?" This lets them process their own thoughts instead of being handed a solution.

3. **Encourage, Don't Eclipse**: Be their cheerleader! Phrases like *"That sounds amazing!"* or *"I love how you're handling this"* affirm their choices and independence.

4. **Listen, Don't Lecture:** Don't say things like, *"I know exactly how you feel,"* or *"Oh, I know exactly what you should do about that."*

5. **Empathize, Don't Minimize:** Work to hear the feelings behind what they're saying. Don't say things like *"Oh, that's no big deal."* Instead, say something like, *"I can see how you'd feel that way."*

By keeping the focus on them by using supportive responses rather than shifting responses, we demonstrate that we value who they are and how they feel.

The next time your child shares something with you, pause before responding.

Will you *shift* the conversation to yourself or *support* them by keeping the focus on them? When you keep the focus on them, you'll see a remarkable difference in their response. They'll be more likely to share with you in the future because they feel supported and heard.

Bob the (Relationship) Builder

> **"A strong relationship with your adult child isn't about control—it's about connection."**
>
> **Unknown**

Did your kids watch the TV show *Bob the Builder* when they were growing up? In the show, Bob and his Can-Do Crew were ready to tackle any project by thinking positively, solving problems, and working together as a team.

How are you going to build your relationship with your adult kids? If the goal of your parenting is friendship, you're going to have to be intentional about it.

First, you've never walked this path before, and neither have they, so you both need to be understanding and patient! You're (hopefully) working hard to see them as young adults with thoughts, ideas, and relationships of their own. Are they also working to see you in a new role? Or are they stuck seeing you as mom?

It's inevitable that you'll make mistakes and fall back into parent mode by accident. After all, giving advice and guidance was your go-to for eighteen years! Likewise, your kids may struggle with defensiveness and hear everything you say as instruction or criticism.

Good friends are trustworthy, loyal, and dependable. They're encouraging, positive, kind, and thoughtful.

We told our kids we would do our best, but we also needed *them* to try to view our relationship differently.

Remember, you're working toward *friendship* with one another. Good friends are trustworthy, loyal, and dependable. They're encouraging, positive, kind, and thoughtful. They're good listeners, nonjudgmental, and express empathy. They're supportive in good times and bad, and they don't give advice unless asked. They respect your time, opinions, and boundaries and are fun to be around. ***Be that person with your kids!***

Make the effort to get on their "turf" and spend one-on-one time with them. Kids *of any age* love to have their parents' undivided attention! I've helped my kids move into new apartments, shopped with them for groceries, and visited their churches when I visited them. Walking through these everyday activities on their turf builds the intimacy of shared experiences. *And that builds relationships.*

Say it with Bob! *"Can we fix it? Yes, we can!"*

Use the space below to write down some practical things you can do to build your relationship with your adult kids. Do those things and *speak it to them* so they know you're working on the relationship. Do things like asking them if you can stock the pantry with their favorite cereal when they come home for the weekend. (By the way, it may have changed from the favorite you remember!) If they're moving, let them know you'd love to help in any way you can, and then do it with a willing heart.

Words Matter

**Death and life are in the power of the
tongue, and those who love it will eat
its fruits.**

Proverbs 18:21 (NASB)

When our kids were little, they bickered occasionally,
just like all siblings.

So, we decided to do a little experiment.

We gave each of them a tube of toothpaste and a paper
plate. We had them squeeze all the toothpaste they
could out onto the plate. Then we told them we would
give $100 to the one who could put all the toothpaste
back into the tube.

They looked at us with big eyes as the fruitlessness of
the situation quickly became apparent.

Words are like toothpaste. Once they're out, you cannot
put them back. Words have *power* and *permanence*.

Do you want your influence in the lives of your (now

adult) children to be that of a Joy Booster—a positive person who uses encouraging words and cheers them on? Or do you want to be a Joy Buster—a negative person who criticizes and tears them down, undermining their confidence and discouraging them?

Joy Boosters energize you with their belief in you. They see and encourage your potential, and they delight in you. Joy Busters do the opposite. They make you feel inadequate and misunderstood.

Which one are you in the life of your adult child?

Parenting adult children is tricky, to say the least. It is *so* easy to slip back into parenting mode and give advice or "suggestions," which are often taken as criticism. At its core, *parenting adult children is mainly about learning to hold your tongue until they invite you into their lives and ask for your input.*

When you've been parenting them one way for the past eighteen-plus years, making the transition to more of a coach and encourager isn't as simple as just flipping a switch!

It's going to take practice, and you're going to fail

sometimes. When you do, ask for forgiveness quickly, and let them know you'll be working harder to think about your words before speaking.

When you do speak, make your words count. Honor and bless them for who they are and what you see as praiseworthy in their lives. (Even if you have to search hard for it!)

You can do it, mama!

Make a list of some things you can encourage in your adult children's lives, so you're ready to be a Joy Booster when you get the opportunity. Use the list below to help you get started.

50 TRAITS YOU CAN ENCOURAGE IN ADULT CHILDREN

1. You're a hard worker.

2. You have a kind heart.

3. You make wise decisions.

4. You're a great problem solver.

5. You have a strong work ethic.

6. You're responsible and dependable.

7. You're thoughtful and considerate.

8. You handle challenges with grace.

9. You're a great listener.

10. You're creative and resourceful.

11. You have a generous spirit.

12. You're courageous and brave.

13. You treat others with respect.

14. You're growing and learning every day.

15. You bring joy to those around you.

16. You're a loyal friend.

17. You see the good in others.

18. You stay true to your values.

19. You're trustworthy and honest.

20. You make people feel valued.

21. You have a great sense of humor.

22. You're independent and capable.

23. You handle responsibilities well.

24. You're compassionate and empathetic.

25. You inspire others with your attitude.

26. You know how to use your resources.

27. You're adaptable and open to change.

28. You put in effort to achieve your goals.

29. You're wise beyond your years.

30. You take initiative and get things done.

31. You make people feel welcome and included.

32. You're thoughtful in your words and actions.

33. You don't give up when things get tough.

34. You bring out the best in others.

35. You're resilient.

36. You have a natural ability to lead.

37. You make decisions with confidence.

38. You're patient and understanding.

39. You're always willing to learn and grow.

40. You face challenges with determination.

41. You respect different perspectives.

42. You're kind and thoughtful.

43. You're sensitive to the needs of others.

44. You're willing to step outside your comfort zone.

45. You know how to find joy in the little things.

46. You're wise in handling money and resources.

47. You encourage and uplift those around you.

48. You take responsibility for your actions.

49. You radiate positivity and optimism.

50. You are deeply loved by many.

When Things Go South

Know this, my beloved brothers: let every person be quick to hear, slow to speak, slow to anger; for the anger of man does not produce the righteousness of God.

James 1:19–20

At some point or another, there will be a misunderstanding with your adult child. It may stem from a conversation that took a wrong turn, unfair expectations, trust issues, or even external stressors. (Um, teenage or midlife hormones, anyone?)

When it happens, take a deep breath and remember—conflict isn't the enemy. In fact, it can be an opportunity for growth, deeper understanding, and even a stronger relationship. The key? Approach the conflict with humility, patience, kindness, and a willingness to listen.

Your role has shifted from hands-on parent to trusted advisor, and that means approaching disagreements with love, grace, and a whole lot of listening. Before jumping in to defend yourself, make excuses, or prove a point, pause . . . What is your adult child really saying? Is there an underlying worry, frustration, or need behind their emotions?

It also helps to ask yourself: *Am I holding onto expectations that don't fit their current stage of life? Did I offer advice or an opinion without being asked? Is my response coming from a place of humility and grace or just wounded feelings?* And most importantly, *how can I handle this in a way that will keep our connection strong?*

Here's what you can do when conversations or situations don't go well:

1. **Be open to their criticism** – Listen non-defensively, and don't explain, make an excuse, rationalize, or push back. Instead, look at the conflict as an opportunity to build greater intimacy and understanding. Even if you feel like they're off base, there is likely *some* truth in what they're saying.

2. **Don't react immediately** – If you're hurt by something your adult child says, take the time you need to humble

and examine yourself. Be a person who
can tolerate criticism, be self-reflective,
and empathize with their feelings.

3. **"Relationship OVER right"** –
   Remember this phrase and repeat it
   to yourself when you feel slighted or
   wronged by something your adult
   child says. Your relationship is more
   important than who is right or wrong.

Use the space below to examine how you feel about conflict. Be honest! Do you see it as something to be avoided at all costs? Or do you see it as a normal, healthy (albeit uncomfortable) part of a mature, mutually respectful relationship? How can you make changes to how you handle it that will help you build a stronger relationship?

"What you do speaks so loudly that I
cannot hear what you say."[17]

Ralph Waldo Emerson

It's easy to use words. But if you really want to nurture
your relationship with your adult children, actions are
where it's at! Here are some practical things you can do
that will enrich and deepen your relationship.

1. **If Something Is a Big Deal to Them,
    Make It a Big Deal to You** – Learn
    enough (on your own) about what
    they love so that you can ask intelligent
    questions. Then *really* listen to their
    answers. Instead of offering advice or
    just passively listening, try to listen for
    the subtext of emotions behind it and
    reflect that back to them. (Is their job
    frustrating? Say something like, *"Ohhh,
    I can see how that must be driving you
    crazy!"*)

2. **Join Them for Activities They Enjoy** – Our daughter is a musical theater actress. When she was growing up, my husband took her to see musicals that came through Dallas on tour. I drove her to and even sat in on many voice, dance, and acting lessons. Through those experiences, we learned an understanding and appreciation for her art form. Now we can talk to her knowledgeably about something that is important to her and ask informed questions. That strengthens our relationship with her.

3. **Pay Them for Their Help** – Your kids' time is valuable, and you want them to know you respect their time and appreciate their skills. When we go out of town, we pay one of our adult kids to either house sit or go by and grab the mail, water plants, and pick up packages. Paying them for their time and efforts is a tangible way to demonstrate that you see them as adults. (Plus, it's a great way to help them out!)

4. **Give Thoughtful Gifts** – Everyone
   loves to get a thoughtful gift! Whether
   it's their favorite candy or a T-shirt
   that would make them laugh, send it
   straight to them from Amazon. In our
   family, we call these "I love you" gifts.
   They don't need an occasion, and they
   always have the recipient in mind.

5. **Show Interest in Their Friends** –
   Whether you're offering to open your
   home for a bridal or baby shower for
   one of your daughter's friends, or just
   asking about how your son's college
   pals are doing now, showing interest in
   their friends will mean a lot to them.
   When our daughter kept bringing
   up the names of her friends and we
   couldn't keep them straight, we asked
   her to create a "friend tree" so we could
   see who knew whom, who was friends
   with whom, and so on. She loved
   this and was truly appreciative of our
   efforts.

6. **Find *Something* to Praise** –
   Undoubtedly, your adult children
   will make choices you don't agree
   with. But even if your relationship

with your adult children is strained,
find *something* to encourage them
about. (You: *"I just wanted you to know,
I love how you look with a beard!"*)

Write down *one* thing you can do today to actively nurture your relationship with your adult kids. It can be as simple as asking about their friends! Do you need to study up on something they love? Send them a thoughtful e-card or another little gift? Do it, mama!

The Blessing of Boundaries

Ready or not, it's time to embrace a beautiful new truth: Your role as a parent has changed. Your kids aren't kids anymore! They're adults. And the healthiest relationships between parents and their grown-up kids are built on a foundation of mutual trust and respect.

If you haven't yet, it's time for a pivot in your parenting role. Rather than focusing on training, correcting, teaching, and directing them like you did when they were younger, your role now looks a whole lot more like supporting, encouraging, and cheering them on from the sidelines.

Healthy boundaries are so important in this season of

parenting! And guess what? Boundaries go both ways!
That means you're going to have to be okay with not
knowing what they're up to and not necessarily agreeing
with all their choices. (I know—easier said than done
sometimes!)

Just like *you're* adjusting to seeing your kids as their own
people, apart from their identity as your children, they
need to adjust to seeing you as your own person, too,
apart from just being Mom. We told our kids that we
were working to view them differently and we asked
that they do the same for us.

Mothering is a sacred calling and a precious privilege,
but if you're an empty nester, it's time to gently remind
yourself (and maybe even your kids!) that your whole
world doesn't revolve around them anymore. (And
that's a good thing for everybody!) You won't always
be available the moment they want to talk, and that's
healthy! It models mutual respect. If they call or text
and you're tied up, try saying, *"I'm busy right now, but*

I'd love to connect later. Here are a few times that would work for me."

It's all about setting expectations—kindly, clearly, and with lots of grace. Make sure your expectations of your kids are reasonable and appropriate, and then be clear with them, whether about visits, finances, or their availability. Ask questions like, *"What works for you?"* instead of assuming. And if they set a boundary that feels hard or even a little bit hurtful, don't take it personally! Boundaries aren't walls—they're bridges to healthier relationships.

And healthy relationships with our adult kids? That's what we're going for!

If you've failed to set appropriate boundaries or respect your adult children's boundaries, then *now* is the time to make things right. Clear the air, forgive (or ask their forgiveness if that's what is needed), and start over. Saying "I'm sorry" and interacting with your adult children from a place of true humility will always be well-received. Jot down your to-do list below and make a plan for when you're going to work through it.

From Mom
to Friend

"The mother-daughter relationship
is a delicate dance of holding on and
letting go."[19]

Amy Bloom

No offense to boy moms, but everyone knows the mother-daughter relationship is *next* level.

Whether it's because of hormones, high expectations, or the natural desire for independence as daughters grow older, the relationship can be extra tricky as you both navigate the next stage of life. Here are five tips that can help you build a strong, intimate relationship with your young adult daughter:

1. **Make It About HER, Not YOU:**
   You're the older, wiser, more mature one, so even if you two are "best friends," remember that you're the *mom* and she is the daughter. As the

younger one, it's expected that she will be more emotionally needy. (If that's not the case, please find a counselor to talk with.) Remember, she doesn't want to hear you complain about her dad and how he snores/chews with his mouth open/has no clue how to use his iPhone, etc.

2. **Acknowledge the Uniqueness of Your Relationship**: Friends will come and go, but Mama has known her *forever!* You've seen her through many ups and downs. The sheer longevity of your relationship allows you the blessing of being the *most unique* friend and emotional support system for her. That's what makes your relationship so valuable.

3. **Be Her Mirror**: With all the emotional and hormonal ups and downs we go through as women, it's helpful to have someone remind us that no matter how intensely we feel at the moment, our current feelings and circumstances will change. Since you've got history together, reminding her of how she felt in a past (similar) situation can be helpful.

4. **Let Her Be the "Expert"**: What is she
   better at than you? Fashion? Ask her
   what she thinks of the latest trends.
   Makeup? Ask her for some tips. She'll
   get to show off a bit, and you'll learn
   a lot. I constantly ask my daughter to
   explain the latest slang to me!

5. **Find Something to Admire, and
   Admire It**: Helping her move?
   Compliment her taste in décor.
   Attending her university's family
   weekend? Tell her how sweet her
   friends are.

At the end of the day, being a girl mom isn't about
getting it perfect! It's about staying connected. Keep
cheering her on, keep showing up, and keep being her
safe place. After all... nobody does "Mom" for her quite
like *you* do.

Use the space below to prepare for your next visit with your daughter. Think in advance about some things you can ask her about or say that will strengthen your bond and write those down so you can refer back to them. Remember to listen more than you speak, and don't shift the conversation onto yourself—even if you're trying to show her you "relate" to her current situation or circumstance.

Adulting 101

One of the greatest joys of the empty nest is seeing your children step into adulthood and become the people they were meant to be.

I love watching my kids navigate school, jobs, relationships, and responsibilities—sometimes stumbling, sometimes soaring. Seeing them succeed in ways big and small brings a sense of fulfillment! ("Ohhh, what we taught them actually *took*! They're amazing!") Their victories, whether landing a first job, managing a budget, or handling a challenging situation with maturity, remind us that every prayer we prayed and every tear we shed was more than worth it.

But as much as their growth brings joy, it can also bring heartache.

Young adulthood is a season of exploration, and sometimes that means our kids will make choices we wouldn't have made, or head down paths we wouldn't have chosen for them. Maybe they've stepped away from family values or the faith that once seemed so sure. Maybe their decisions feel unwise, risky, or even heartbreaking, with potentially long-term consequences. And sometimes, there can even be estrangement, for short or long periods, leaving you feeling helpless and heartbroken.

When the road they take or the choices they make aren't the ones you envision, it can be tempting to step in—but, unless it's a matter of health or safety, you need to resist. Part of loving your adult children well is allowing them the space to grow, learn, and even fail.

With adult children, you're not in the driver's seat anymore, and that's as it should be. Remember, learning to be the parent of an adult involves an entirely different skill set than parenting did when they were younger.

But never doubt this for a second: Your role in their lives is still as important as ever.

No matter how old they are, children crave the
encouragement of their parents. Know that your
kindness, unconditional love, and continued prayers
make a difference for them.

Reflect on your child's journey into adulthood.
What qualities do you admire most about
them? If there are struggles or disappointments,
how can you shift from worry to prayer or
encouragement? (see 1 Peter 5:7) Use the space
below to write down a few practical ways
you can show them love and support in this
season, even if their path looks different than
what you expected.

Bridging the Conversation Gap

**Kind words are like honey—sweet to
the soul and healthy for the body.**

Proverbs 16:24 (NLT)

Want to have meaningful conversations with your
adult kids? We *all* do! Unfortunately, it's not as easy
as it sounds! The road to good communication and
meaningful conversation with your adult kids can be
strewn with potential pitfalls and landmines.

It's challenging to shift from parenting, character
training, giving advice, and offering "suggestions."
Right? After all, you spent eighteen-plus years doing
just that! As challenging as it is for you, know that it's
difficult for your adult kids as well. Just as you've always
seen them as children in need of parenting, advice, and
instruction, they've always seen you in the role of parent
(the giver of all those things)!

Altering that mindset isn't like flipping a light switch for either of you, which is what can make things tricky. Doing it well requires intentionality, humility, self-control, and thoughtfulness.

Even if you work on *not* parenting when you talk to your adult kids, because of the roles you've always played in each other's lives, they can often *hear* what you say through the paradigm of parenting.

Your *observations* and *questions* may sound like criticism to their ears, and your *suggestions* may sound like you don't have confidence in their ability to run their own lives.

So, where do you start? Begin with the end in mind and work backward! Start by thinking through your goal for the relationship. For us it was *friendship*.

Just like you, as we raised our kids, we kept in mind that we were their *parents*, and not their *friends*. Still, the goal of our parenting was friendship with them (and our prayer was that they turned out to be people we *wanted* to be friends with).

Write out your goals for your relationship with each of your adult kids. Do you need to heal old wounds? Reconcile from estrangement? Or just deepen an already strong relationship? Read James 1:19 and 1:26 and be honest with yourself and the Lord about where you may need to make changes in your communication. Use the space below.

**Let your speech always be
gracious, seasoned with salt, so that
you may know how you ought to
answer each person.**

Colossians 4:6

Houston, we have a problem.

We don't know how to ask good questions.

Whether you're trying to make new friends at midlife
or trying to get the scoop on your kids' out-of-the-nest
lives, you need to learn how to ask good questions
(without being invasive). Oh, it's a danger zone for sure!

The wrong questions can turn a situation that should
be all about someone else into one that is all about you.
The right questions can lay the foundation for a more
connected, trusting relationship.

Be encouraged! Once you've really looked at where

you might have gone wrong in past conversations, it's time to move forward. There *are* things you can do to navigate this tricky road with your adult children proactively. Remember that it's about showing genuine interest and creating a space where your adult children (or friends!) feel safe sharing what's really going on in their lives without feeling judged.

- **Have an open and honest conversation** about the relationship you want to have with them and humbly ask forgiveness for times when you may have veered off course in the past. (Be specific about these times and ask for "forgiveness" instead of just saying, *"I'm sorry."* Forgiveness carries a lot more weight.)

- **Learn to ask good questions.** The wrong questions can be perceived as criticism (especially by your kids). But the right questions can support, encourage, and lead to a deeper, more intimate conversation. Open-ended questions are ideal because they invite further discussion. For example, instead of *"Did you have a good day?"* ask, *"What was the best part of your day today?"* or *"Tell me* *about something that made you laugh today."*

- **Be mindful of your tone and timing**. Respecting their emotional state and their comfort level is crucial. For example, instead of saying, *"Why don't you ever call me?"* (which might come off as guilt-laden), try asking, *"What are the best ways for us to stay connected?"*

- **Be honest about the challenges** of shifting the way you view each other's roles and acknowledge that it will take some adjustment and work.

- **Do not give advice unless asked for it**—and even then, keep it brief and ask them what they think about the advice. Sometimes, when I *truly* believe I have something especially meaningful to share, I say something like, *"I have a* *thought! Do you want to hear it? You can say no."* (They almost never will, but if they do, you *have* to be okay with that.)

- **Keep the focus on them**. When they share something, don't fall into the (very common) trap of bringing up a similar situation from your own life. (Remember the shift response.)

- **Work on your listening skills**. When you listen, do it with your *heart*, empathetically "hearing" what your adult kids are saying. Don't spend the time when they're talking thinking of your response. Remember, you can't say the wrong thing if you're listening, and fewer words are almost always better.

- **Do what you can to emphasize the longevity and intimate nature of your parent/child relationship**. It's special and unique! You *literally* saw them grow up, and because of this, you may be able to share helpful information about their childhood. My adult son is a good friend to those in need. He *loved* it when I told him that

he was *always* a good friend and shared
some stories from his childhood that
illustrated that.

- **Do something together that you
both enjoy**. This will prompt easy,
organic conversation.

- **Watch their face and body language**.
If your questions start to irritate them,
move on to another topic.

- **Be positive and encouraging**. Ask
thoughtful and intelligent follow-up
questions and find honest, uplifting
comments to make. Use phrases like,

  - *That's amazing!*

  - *I always knew you'd be good at
____________.*

  - *I am completely in awe of you!*

  - *Congratulations. That's
phenomenal!*

  - *I'm so proud of you!*

Write out your plan for improving your communication with your adult children. Which of the items above do you need to work on the most? Be honest. Then ask the Lord for help.

Therefore encourage one another and build one another up, just as you are doing.

1 Thessalonians 5:11

Conversation with your adult kids might look a little different than it did back in the days of carpools, curfews, and catching up over chicken nuggets at the kitchen table! These days, it takes a little more intention, a little more creativity (and sometimes a little more patience) to stay connected in meaningful ways.

But, oh friend, let me encourage you: it is *so* worth the effort.

Your grown-up kids still want to feel known and loved by you (even if they don't always say it out loud). And one of the sweetest ways to nurture that connection is by asking thoughtful, open-ended questions—the kind that show you care not just about what they *do*, but about who they *are*.

These kinds of thoughtful questions help you go beyond surface-level small talk and invite your child to share their heart, their dreams, their challenges, and their joys. They say, "I see you. I'm for you. I love being part of your world, and I'm invested."

Here are a few to try:

1. *Tell me about* ____________________*?*
   Asking intelligent questions about their areas of expertise allows them to be the expert! Let them tell you about their job, their career field, and why they love it.

2. *What do you think about* __________________*?*

3. *What does a typical day look like for you?*
   We used this around the dinner table with two of our adult kids a few months ago, and they loved sharing their days and hearing about each other's days as well.

4. *How is*____________*?*
   My kids are always grateful when I remember names and ask about their friends.

5. *Whatever happened with* _______________*?* (Fill in the blank with a situation they mentioned a while ago but never followed up on with you.)

6. *What do you remember about* _______________*?* (Fill in the blank about something from their upbringing. There's nothing wrong with a quick reminder of your shared family history!)

7. *How did you know how to handle* _________ *or what to do?* (Fill in the blank with a person/situation.) This will show them that you admire and respect them, and want to learn from them. Plus, it will set you up to encourage them!

8. Ask their advice—and be sure to tell them what it is about them that makes you specifically want their advice. (This demonstrates that you realize your relationship is evolving and acknowledges that they have wisdom to share that is valuable to you.)

If you're making changes from old patterns of communication, learning to use conversation starters may take practice. Ask a friend out for lunch or coffee and work on it. Remember to keep the focus on them.

50 Conversation Starters for Young Adult Kids

1. What's the best movie you've ever seen and why?

2. What's your favorite app on your phone and why?

3. Walk me through a typical day in your life.

4. What's your primary love language? Where do the others rank for you?

5. If you could time travel, what era would you visit and why?

6. What's the best advice you've ever received?

7. What's an unpopular opinion you have?

8. What has the Lord been teaching you lately?

9. What's the worst style choice you've ever made?

10. What's your favorite thing about being the age you are? Least favorite?

11. What's a guilty pleasure song you listen to regularly?

12. If you were stranded on a deserted island, what's the one thing you would bring?

13. What's the best way to spend a rainy day and why?

14. What's your favorite childhood memory?

15. What makes you nervous?

16. What book has had the most impact on your life?

17. What's one thing you wish people knew about you?

18. Finish this sentence: "I wish I knew how to _______."

19. What's the best compliment you've ever received?

20. What advice would you give your younger self?

21. What's your favorite time of day and why?

22. What's one moment in your life you'd love to relive?

23. Finish this sentence: "I'm happiest when ________."

24. When you picture your future in 10 years, what do you see?

25. What recurring dream do you have?

26. What do you miss most about childhood?

27. What teacher has had the most impact on your life and why?

28. What's your favorite Bible verse and why?

29. If money were no object, where would you like to travel and why?

30. What does the term "success" mean to you?

31. Which three positive words best describe you?

32. If you had $100 to spend today, what would you buy?

33. What's the one thing you want to accomplish in your lifetime?

34. What's the most adventurous thing you've ever done?

35. Which of your friends do you admire most and why?

36. What's the strangest food you've ever eaten?

37. What's your favorite season and why?

38. What's something small that can really make your day?

39. What's something you wouldn't want to change about yourself?

40. How often do you give yourself permission to relax? Why?

41. Describe yourself in five words.

42. What's your most treasured possession and why?

43. What's been the highlight of your week so far and why?

44. What's one thing you're really looking forward to in the next few months?

45. What's something that's challenged you lately, and how are you handling it?

46. Is there a habit or routine you've developed recently that's really helped you?

47. What's something small that made you smile this week?

48. Who is the most difficult
    person in your life to deal
    with and why?

49. What's a skill you've picked
    up that you never expected
    to learn?

50. What's the biggest thing
    you've learned about
    yourself since leaving
    home?

"If ever there is tomorrow when we're
not together... there is something
you must always remember. You are
braver than you believe, stronger
than you seem, and smarter than you
think. But the most important thing
is, even if we're apart...
I'll always be with you."[21]

Winnie-the-Pooh

All relationships need space to breathe, and yet they also take intentionality to grow! Just because your adult kids have launched doesn't mean they don't still need you. (Spoiler alert: they do!) It just looks a little different now.

Staying close when you don't get to see them face-to-face as often as you'd like takes intentionality, thoughtfulness, and a little creativity. You can do it, mama!

So, how can you stay close to your adult kids when you don't get to see them face-to-face as often as you'd like? Here are five meaningful things that you can do to keep your relationship thriving.

1. **Digital Communication**: Your kids are just a text, a FaceTime, or a phone call away! Take the time to send funny articles, quotes, or memes to your kids, and react appropriately when they send one back. If they're sick, check on them at least once a day to see how they're feeling, or have some chicken noodle soup delivered to them from their local grocery store.

2. **Get on Their Turf**: When you get on their turf, you'll learn so much about them! Showing you where they work, attend school, or even grocery shop is important to them! Seeing all of that will give you insight into their everyday lives.

3. **Help Practically When You Can:** When your kids ask you for help, GO! If they need help moving, recovering

from mononucleosis, driving cross-country, or getting over a bad breakup, GO!

4. **Love Who They Love:** The young women my sons have married are different from me—and that's a *good* thing! I don't focus on our differences, I focus on our similarities, and the biggest one of all—they love my sons. If you struggle with your relationship with your child's significant other, remember, you're the grown-up, and it's up to you to set the tone! Take your eyes off yourself and focus on what you have in common—love for your son (or daughter). Don't let your personal expectations (there's that word again!) color your relationship with them. Pray for them and ask the Lord to show you how you can serve and bless them.

5. **Get Familiar with Their Friends:** Your kids' friends are *very* important to them. Learn their names, remember the things your kids tell you about them, and ask about them when you

spend time with your kids. After asking
about his friends one day, my son (who
is not typically a big compliment-
giver), told me he really appreciated
that I did this!

Use the space below to make a list of some practical ways you can stay close to your adult kids who live far away. Then make a plan to implement one of them *today*.

Love in Action

My little children, let us not love in word or in tongue, but in deed and in truth.

1 John 3:18 (NKJV)

Want to do a better job of showing love to your adult children? No matter what age they are, your kids need to know you love them. It's just as true when they leave home as it was when they were in the nest! Your expressions of love are going to look different, for sure, but it's more important than ever that you show them your approval and love.

Here are a few practical things you can do:

1. **Be Their Cheerleader** – Everybody needs an attaboy sometimes, and your adult kids need to know that you have full confidence in them and in their ability to handle challenges and adversity. Say things like, *"You've got this! It may be challenging, but because*

*you're the kind of person that _______(list
positive character qualities here)_______,
I know you've got what it takes to handle
this."*

2. **Be Generous** – I'm not necessarily
   talking about money! Be generous with
   your time, your resources, and your
   support.

3. **Keep Your Opinions to Yourself
   (Mostly)** – Suzy suggests NO
   "suggestions!" The growing-up process
   can look like a hot mess! Growth
   includes pain, and you can't always
   smooth the way for those you love. It
   will be hard to watch sometimes but
   resist the urge to make "suggestions" or
   intervene (unless it's a matter of safety).

4. **Be a Good Listener** – Always ask about
   them first. Say things like, *"How was
   your day? How did everything work out
   with ___(situation, person)___?"* Let
   them talk and listen empathetically

with your heart. Do not go into a
conversation with a needy agenda or
unrealistic expectations!

5. **Speak It** – *Tell* them you love them. If
   they're embarrassed, shorten it to *"Love
   ya!"* and say it *even more* often!

6. **Pray for Them** – Pray for your kids
   and tell them that you're praying for
   them.

Think through the list above and use the space below to work through any changes or shifts you may need to make.

Hope When They Wander

Train up a child in the way he should go; even when he is old he will not depart from it.

Proverbs 22:6 (NKJV)

You pray it won't happen with your kids. But it might.

When your children leave the nest, they'll be exposed to new thoughts, temptations, values, and ways of life. Culture will bombard them with the things of this world (1 John 2:15). It's a lot to work through.

You took them to church faithfully and worked diligently to cultivate a durable faith, but now they're doubting and struggling. Don't blame yourself. As they become adults, their faith must become their own.

If your young adult children are questioning (or have abandoned) the faith they were raised in, you may feel helpless. What should you do?

1. **Live Out God's Word.** Don't be preachy or nag! They will eventually tune you out, and it will harm your relationship. Instead, continue to live out your faith. The way they see you love others and live your life is your most powerful witness.

2. **Be Ready If They Bring It Up**. If they bring up their doubts, your initial reaction may be to feel anxious, afraid, or even defensive. Instead, be sensitive, respectful, loving, and understanding. If you want to continue the conversation, they need to feel safe and comfortable sharing their thoughts and feelings with you.

3. **Strive for a Loving, Open Discussion** where you will do more prayerful listening than talking. Be honest about your own doubts and struggles and assure them of your unconditional love for them.

4. **Pray, Pray, Pray.** Pray for your adult children to find truth, peace, and strength in their faith, Also, pray for yourself. Pray that God gives you the faith to hand over your child to Him,

knowing that you have done your best. Know that the Lord is up for the task of wooing their hearts. It may be hard to comprehend, but He loves them **even more** than you do!

If you're going through this with your adult child, know that you're not alone and don't give in to shame or blame. Instead, reach out to a good friend, a pastor, or a mentor who can listen and pray with you. Do it today.

When They Hurt, You Hurt

Rejoice with those who rejoice, weep with those who weep.

Romans 12:15

Whether your adult kids are dealing with a bad breakup, an injury, or illness, or even something as traumatic as the death of a friend or spouse, as parents we *desperately* want to help. What is the best way to help when your adult children are struggling or in a time of crisis without overstepping? Here are 10 things you can do.

1. **Stay Connected**: Staying in touch on a regular basis builds your relationship and makes you the natural person for them to reach out to when things get tough.

2. **Listen Without Judgement**: Create a safe space for them to share and listen

without distractions. Let them feel
heard. Resist the urge to jump in with
judgment or solutions.

3. **Reflect Their Feelings**: Empathize
   and reflect their feelings in a genuine
   way. If they're crying and you feel teary,
   cry with them.

4. **Don't Make It About You**: Don't say,
   "I know exactly how you feel," or tell
   them about the time something similar
   happened to you. You may be trying to
   establish rapport or let them know that
   you understand their feelings, but trust
   me, you don't.

5. **Respect Their Independence**: They
   need to make their own decisions and
   learn from their mistakes. Offer advice
   only when asked.

6. **Pray for Them:** Praying for your adult
   children is the most crucial thing you
   can do for them (see Philippians 4:5-7).

7. **Help Practically**: If asked, be *physically*
   present. When my adult daughter tore
   ligaments in her ankle and had to be
   non-weight-bearing for a week, I flew

to another state to help her. I drove her
to work, cleaned her house, did her
laundry, and cooked.

8. **If You're Not Sure How to Help, Ask**:
   Your instinct may be to rush in and fix
   everything, but asking how best to help
   rather than assuming shows respect for
   them as adults.

9. **Utilize Helpful Resources**: If your
   adult child is dealing with a crisis
   like a life-threatening diagnosis or
   a hospitalization, consider asking
   a friend for help or using a helpful
   online resource to keep others
   informed. (But only if you have
   permission.)

10. **Stay Engaged:** Even after a crisis has
    passed, the struggle can be ongoing!
    Regular check-ins via text or call can
    provide ongoing support without being
    intrusive.

It can hurt when adult kids turn to friends or even other family members in a time of crisis, but remember not to make it about yourself. You're the grown-up! Follow the tips, regardless of *your* feelings. Take a moment to jot down and pray through where you might need to humbly make changes in your approach.

Find the Funny

**God will yet fill your mouth
with laughter and your lips
with shouts of joy.**

Job 8:21–22 (NIV)

Laughter really *is* one of the best ways to stay close when life is busy, schedules are full, and everyone's spread out in different directions (or time zones!). Humor has a beautiful way of melting away awkwardness, bridging generational gaps, lightening the mood, and reminding us all not to take life—or ourselves—too seriously.

A shared laugh turns ordinary conversations into inside jokes, and inside jokes into memorable moments that last for years to come.

Of course, the *best* humor is *always* kind. Teasing that's gentle and good-natured builds connection, but if the punchline comes at someone's expense, it's time to skip that joke. (Remember: Laughter should leave everyone smiling, not stinging.)

Here are some playful, lighthearted ways to sprinkle humor into your relationship with your adult kids.

1. **Find Your Shared Sense of Humor**: Remind everyone about funny shared memories that live on in family lore—those that make everyone laugh until they cry.

2. **Laugh at Yourself**: Showing your fun-loving side and being able to laugh at yourself is so important! One day, when my husband and I were sleep-deprived with a new baby and potty training another little one, my husband excused himself from a business meeting by saying, "I'll be right back, I need to go potty!" This has gone down in his company's time-honored stories, not to mention our family lore!

3. **Engage in Their World**: If your adult child loves a particular comedy show or podcast, tune in! Then say something like, "I finally listened to that podcast you love, and wow—that was wild!" It will give you something new to share or laugh about together.

4. **Create New "Inside Jokes" Together**: This could be as simple as giving each other silly nicknames or referencing something funny from a recent conversation.

5. **Laugh Through Life's Awkward Moments:** My kids are always up for a story about when I do something awkward! When I told them about signing an email to an important person, "Best, Suxy," because I was typing too fast, they died of laughter.

6. **Turn Small Moments Into Lighthearted Fun:** Don't underestimate the power of humor in everyday moments. Text them a funny meme you saw or tell a funny story from your day. It doesn't have to be anything fancy; even a lighthearted *"Good morning, sunshine!"* text can brighten their day and remind them they're loved.

7. **Laugh *with* Them:** When your kids are playful with you, respond! If they share something funny with you, respond with laughing emojis or GIFs to show them you get the joke.

Staying connected through humor is as much about the small, consistent touches as it is about big, laugh-out-loud moments. Everyone loves a good audience! When your kids know you're a source of positivity and fun, they'll keep coming back for more.

LIVE IT OUT

When something funny happens,
make it a habit to stop right then to share it with
one of your kids who would enjoy it.
Shared humor builds intimacy.

Sweet empty-nester mama, if you've made it to the end of this book, that tells me something beautiful about you—you *want* to find joy in your empty nest. You want to live with purpose, walk in faith, and be the best parent you can be to your adult kids. I am so proud of you for that. And I believe with all my heart that the Lord will honor the desires of your heart (see Psalm 37:4).

Will it always be easy? Nope. But stay faithful. Stay humble. Stay persistent. Rest in the good work you did when your children were under your roof and release them into God's capable hands. He will never leave you or forsake you (see Isaiah 41:10).

I wrote *Empty Nest Blessed: 60 Days to Finding Joy in the Empty Nest* to speak to both your heart and your mind. I designed it to be active—so you wouldn't just read, but engage. I made it pretty so you'd want to leave it out and come back to it often. And I made it comprehensive so you could return to it again and again, through the seasons and stages of this new chapter.

The empty nest season is full of change and challenge,

yes—but it's also overflowing with discovery, growth, purpose, and delight. There is freedom here. There is fun. And there is so, so much joy.

I hope you'll continue the journey with me at EmptyNestBlessed.com, where we cheer each other on and cover everything from fashion and beauty to faith, travel, wellness, parenting, and more. My heart is to encourage, inspire, and *bless* you—to be your encourager in this sweet season of life.

You've got this, friend. Keep walking in faith. Keep choosing joy. And remember—this season, like all others, is just that: a season. But the goodness of God? That never changes.

I'm right here with you—heart to heart, hand in hand, trusting the Lord, and joyfully living it out.

To my precious husband: Thank you for rejoicing with me, listening so patiently to my ideas, steadying me when I need it, and faithfully serving me and our family every single day. Your joy is contagious, and making you laugh is one of my favorite things in life! You love me so well. Every day, I marvel at God's tremendous love poured out when He gave *you* to *me* and allowed me to do life by your side.

To my sweet kids, who first made me a mama—and then an empty nester: Thank you for your prayers, your grace, and your patience. I adore you more than words can say! Mothering you has been the greatest privilege of my life, and watching you grow into the young adults God created you to be is my greatest joy (3 John 1:4). You three know better than anyone how often I've stumbled in living out the very advice I've shared in this book! But I promise you this: I will keep trying my best until my final breath. I love you so much.

To my darling daughters-in-law: What a gift you are! The Lord didn't make me your mother (you each have amazing parents who poured into you with love and prayer), but He *surprised me with joy* when He added you to our family. Thank you for loving my sweet sons so beautifully and becoming such precious additions to our family. And thank you for making me a LouLou to those adorable grandchildren—they are pure delight!

To my parents: Thank you for your love, your prayers, and for always making sure we found a church home as we moved from place to place. Your encouragement and support have meant the world to me, and I've always longed to make you proud! Even now, your encouragement means more than you know.

To my siblings, in-laws, and extended family: Thank you for the love and support you show to me and my family! Whether it's through your encouragement, thoughtful invitations, or simply cheering on my kids and grandkids in your own special ways, your presence in their lives (and mine) is such a blessing. I'm so thankful to have you as part of my story.

To my right-hand girl, Beth: If you had a dollar for every time I told you I couldn't write this book without you… Well, let's just say you'd be sipping a latte on a beach somewhere! Thank you for cheering me on, listening to my endless stream of ideas, and carrying the load at *EmptyNestBlessed.com* so I could focus on writing. You started as a follower, became an employee, and ended up a dear, dear friend. I'm beyond grateful for you.

To my joyfully creative friend, Steph: Thank you for pushing me (with love!) to finally say yes to writing this book. Your enthusiasm, your can-do spirit, and your unwavering belief in me kept me going. Thank you for checking in on me again and again, and for being the ultimate hype girl. I can't wait to return the favor someday, sweet friend!

To the amazing community of empty nesters I've had the joy of connecting with—whether through blog posts, social media, speaking engagements, interviews, or in person: Thank you for every message, every comment, every story you've shared. You are a tremendous blessing to me, and the reason I do what I do with such joy.

And most of all…

To my Jesus: Thank You for Your love and grace poured out in my life. You saved me, You sustain me, and You continue to gently remind me every day that I am Yours. You are the reason I could write a single word. You worked out every detail of my life so perfectly, and my greatest desire is to honor and give glory to you with my every thought, word, and deed. I fall so short, but you pour out your abundant grace in my life moment by moment. I continue to be amazed by all the times I went to bed with questions and woke up knowing exactly what to write (Psalm 16:7). Thank you for faithfully and abundantly answering every one of the million "Help me, Jesus" prayers I prayed as I wrote and edited! You are my everything.

Notes

1   Alexander Pope, from a letter to John Gay, October 6, 1727.

2   Christopher N Cascio et al, "Self-Affirmation Activates Brain System Associated with Self-Related Processing and Reward and Is Reinforced by Future Orientation." Social Cognitive and Affective Neuroscience, Volume 11, Issue 4, (April 2016): 621–629, https://doi.org/10.1093/scan/nsv136

3   Unknown, "The Real Health Benefits of Smiling and Laughing," Intermountain Health, https://intermountainhealthcare.org/blogs/the-real-health-benefits-of-smiling-and-laughing. Updated Apr 1, 2024.

4   This quote is widely attributed to Stormie Omartian, but no primary source has been located. It may reflect a paraphrasing of ideas from her book The Power of Praying for Your Adult Children (Eugene, Oregon: Harvest House Publishers, 2014).

5   This quote is widely attributed to Carin Rubenstein, but no primary source has been

located. It may reflect a paraphrasing of ideas from her book *Beyond the Mommy Years: How to Live Happily Ever After . . . After the Kids Leave Home* (New York: Hachette Books, 2007)

6   Bishop T.D. Jakes (@BishopJakes), "If you can't figure out your purpose, figure out your passion. For your passion will lead you right into your purpose." X, July 9, 2019

7   Theodore Roosevelt, quoted by Serge Faldin in "Teddy Roosevelt: Do What You Can, With What You Have, Where You Are," Medium, November 5, 2020. https://sfaldin.medium.com/teddy-roosevelt-do-what-you-can-with-what-you-have-where-you-are-b34c5c60649a

8   Eleanor Roosevelt, Forbes Quotes, https://www.forbes.com/quotes/2610/

9   This quote is widely attributed to Eleanor Roosevelt, but no primary source has been located.

10   Mignon McLaughlin, *The Second Neurotic's Notebook* (New York: Bobbs-Merrill, 1966).

11   This quote is widely attributed to Chuck Swindoll, but no primary source has been located. It may reflect a paraphrasing of ideas

from his book *Marriage: From Surviving to Thriving* (Nashville, TN: Thomas Nelson, 2008)

12   Michael Altschuler, "The Bad News is time flies. The Good News is you're the pilot," Goodreads, accessed April 16, 2025, https://www.goodreads.com/quotes/144299

13   Stephen R. Covey, *The 7 Habits of Highly Effective People: Powerful Lessons in Personal Change* (New York: Free Press, 2004)

14   C.S. Lewis, *The Four Loves* (New York: Harcourt, 1960)

15   This quote is widely attributed to Mel Robbins, but no primary source has been located. It may reflect a paraphrasing of ideas from her podcast *The Mel Robbins Show.*

16   Jim Burns Ph.D., *Doing Life with Your Adult Children: Keep Your Mouth Shut and the Welcome Mat Out* (Nashville, TN: Zondervan, 2019)

17   This quote is widely attributed to Ralph Waldo Emerson, though no primary source has been located. It likely reflects a paraphrasing from his 1875 essay "Social Aims" where he wrote: "Don't say things. What you are stands over you the while, and thunders so that I cannot hear what you say to the contrary."

18   Nedra Glover Tawwab, *Set Boundaries, Find Peace: A Guide to Reclaiming Yourself* (New York: Tarcher Publishing, 2021)

19   This quote is widely attributed to Amy Bloom but no primary source could be found. It could reflect a paraphrasing of her ideas from her article, "Mothers and Daughters: Are You Overstepping Your Boundaries?" published by Oprah.com.

20   Elisabeth Elliot, *The Shaping of a Christian Family* (Nashville, TN: Thomas Nelson, 1992).

21   Carter Crocker (Writer) and Karl Geurs (Director), *Pooh's Grand Adventure: The Search for Christopher Robin* (Burbank, CA: Walt Disney Home Video, 1997)